MOBILITY
OF
IMAGINATION

DRAGAN KLAIC

MOBILITY
OF
IMAGINATION

A companion guide
to international cultural cooperation

CENTER FOR ARTS AND CULTURE
CENTRAL EUROPEAN UNIVERSITY

Published by

Center for Arts and Culture
Central European University

Zrínyi utca 14, H-1051 Budapest, Hungary
Tel: (+36-1) 327-3863
Fax: (+36-1) 327-3809
E-mail: cac@ceu.hu
Website: www.cac.ceu.hu

In conjunction with Euclid, UK and the Budapest Observatory

Distributed by

Central European University Press
Budapest – New York
Nádor utca 11, H-1051 Budapest, Hungary
Tel: (+36-1) 327-3138
Fax: (+36-1) 327-3183
E-mail: ceupress@ceu.hu
Website: http://www.ceupress.com

400 West 59th Street, New York NY 10019, USA
Telephone (+1-212) 547-6932, Fax: (+1-646) 557-2416
E-mail: mgreenwald@sorosny.org

Publication of this book was made possible by SICA
Website: http://www.sica.nl

ISBN 978-963-9776-06-7

Library of Congress Cataloging-in-Publication Data
Klaic, Dragan.
  Mobility of imagination : a companion guide to international cultural cooperation / Dragan Klaic. – 1st ed.
    p. cm.
  Includes bibliographical references.
  ISBN 978-9639776067 (pbk.: alk. paper)
  1. Arts–Europe–International cooperation. 2. International relations and culture–Europe. I. Title.
NX705.K53 2007
303.48'24–dc22
                                2007029561

Cover design by Éva Szalay – Skicc and Skicc
Typography and layout by Béla Vetula – Vetula Visual Bt.
Printed in Hungary by GMN Repro Studio

CONTENTS

INTRODUCTION

This book has been written in response to the expressed needs of many students and emerging cultural operators, who desire to engage in international cultural cooperation, seek to define their starting position and to acquire a clear understanding of benefits and risks of international work. They observe the growing internationalization of cultural life around them, but in order to become professionally engaged themselves, they need information, networks, skills, insights and some internalized values and beliefs.

People already working in cultural organizations tend to engage in international projects with great enthusiasm, but often encounter difficulties, dilemmas and even critical situations that crop up as a consequence of their inexperience, a wrong choice of partners, inadequate planning and budgeting or a range of unexpected factors that can turn nice plans into painful disappointments.

The following chapters should hopefully help square ambitions and resources, balance expectations and practical circumstances and bring a range of critical issues into focus of the steady attention of cultural operators. Even then, international cultural cooperation remains a risky endeavor, especially for the small and fragile cultural organizations with more drive than means.

Instead of some theoretical or historical approach, derived from cultural studies, political science, sociology or international relations, this book offers the prospective cultural professional a systematic overview of practical steps, phases, aspects and issues to be mastered in developing and implementing international cultural cooperation projects. A range of practical experiences and concrete examples are invoked from various cultural sectors and artistic disciplines, and different countries of Europe. Concepts are clarified and some key words defined in the glossary. The accent is clearly on cultural cooperation within Europe, where, over the last 60–70 years, extensive cultural systems have been developed as a part of public policy, through public investment, and public authorities regularly appear as instigators and financiers of international cultural cooperation.

The material in this book is organized to cover the basic needs of the user, regardless of country of residence, and despite substantial differences that do exist among national cultural systems and traditions in Europe. Those differences are taken into account, but Europe is seen here as a large emerging cultural space, encompassing not just the 27 members states of the European Union but also South-Eastern and Eastern Europe and the Caucasus, and thus also including such formidable potential partners as those in Russia and Turkey. Cultural cooperation with partners outside Europe is also considered, especially in the neighborhood of the continent, in the Southern Mediterranean, for instance. This expanded field clearly implicates additional complexity and some specific cultural, political and geo-strategic issues.

Even though this reference book is aimed primarily at practitioners—those cultural operators engaged directly in not-for-profit international projects—a major part of the book will hopefully be of some use to other involved parties as well: public officials, staff of private foundations, members and officers of cultural and professional associations, board members of cultural organizations, cultural diplomats, cultural researchers, policy makers and journalists. This is not just a technical guide—not only because it inevitably expresses the personal experiences, convictions and beliefs of its author, but also because when it comes to culture, and especially in the arts, personal affinities, taste, judgment and motivation play a crucial role. With all their diversity and originality, specific international projects actually emerge where personal vision, talent and expertise work in conjunction with institutional and systemic capacities, regulations and standards.

The book is written for enterprising individuals and strives to enhance their performance in an institutional situation, within national cultural systems, and especially in instances where those systems interact. The scope of the book is intentionally modest, but a list of suggested reading and some internet references will lead the inquisitive reader to additional sources of information and to lively debates of practitioners, researchers and decision makers about various facets, the direction and impact of international cultural cooperation today, and its meaning for the construction of Europe as an integrated public sphere, cultural market and creative realm.

Amsterdam, June 2007

1

CULTURES BEYOND BORDERS

Cultural interactions and influences tend to override locality and stretch across borders of language, culture, ethnicity and state. Local cultural expressions and cultural goods are affected by influences coming from far away, and cultural production tends to be dynamic and mobile. Since antiquity, European cultural expressions have been shaped by the influences derived from the greater Mediterranean basin and Asia Minor. Greeks borrowed from the Balkans and Asia, Romans borrowed from the Greeks, Byzantium borrowed from the East, and early Christian culture of the Middle Age reflected intensive migration and conquest. Wars, commerce and migration have been transmitting cultural influences for centuries, more by force than in a cooperative manner. A constant hybridization of cultural production makes claims of authenticity or cultural purity with regard to some specific cultural goods untenable. Christianity, as a religious system, has been uniting and dividing European people, but also offering a framework for intellectual and creative interactions. Thanks to Islamic mediators, the cultures of ancient Greece and Rome reached the savants of Christian Europe and prompted the Renaissance shifts in conceptualization of human individuality.

Printing and the techniques of engraving facilitated a Europe-wide dissemination of ideas and images. Renaissance humanism, the Baroque, Enlightenment and Romanticism were all cultural movements and aesthetic trends that transcended the boundaries of region, state, culture and language, interconnecting various creative centers in Europe. Writers, artists and craftsmen kept traveling throughout Europe, seeking to learn new skills, create and follow fashions, as well as to find patrons and customers. Universities attracted an international cast of prominent scientists who in turn attracted students from great distances. Merchants spread their products widely, and already in the Renaissance some cities had reputations as prominent cultural centers, which attracted foreigners, while the fame of some individual artists reached European proportions, eliciting invitations from aristocratic patrons far afield and circles of international followers and pupils. Italian composers were frequently appointed court composers and Kapellmeisters, and many Italian, Dutch and Flemish painters worked across Europe.

Common cultural traits

A sense of *common European culture* was shaped in the Renaissance and reinforced during the Enlightenment, to be spread further by the expansion of the ideas of the French Revolution and the ensuing Romantic movement. In the beginning of the 19th century, Romanticism articulated the notions of folk culture and national culture, the sense of cultural specificity of place, region and nation (language, oral literature, folklore, customs) and yet, at the same time, it reiterated similar cultural markers and accented the same set of motives, figures and topoi in distinct cultural realms across Europe. Programs of *national* emancipation, liberation and independence connected distinct cultural segments and zones, while the mass exile of national liberation fighters and free thinkers due to repression, furthered cultural interactions and mutual influences in many of the places of exile as well as within the diasporic communities.

Rulers, aristocrats and rich burghers, city councils and later governments have been establishing *cultural institutions* for their own glory and public benefit since the 17th and 18th centuries: libraries, museums and galleries, learned societies, opera houses and theater companies, concert halls and orchestras, archives and journals. Their impact was originally local or national, but some of them achieved an international reputation and set intellectual and professional standards of Europe-wide significance. Some of these institutions established international contacts and relations with their peers, received foreign visitors and presented their work, thus encouraging international mobility among cultural professionals and of cultural goods, and furthering their appreciation abroad. How these institutions were established, the timing, manner and process, reflects the divergence of cultural and political circumstances in Europe, and even today, some evident differences in the position and functioning of cultural institutions can be traced back to the circumstances of their founding, more than 200 years ago.

Nation, ideology and politics

The emergence of the *nation state* and its utilization of culture to build a distinct national identity showed a striving to accent cultural differences and sharpen the distinctions among various cultural realms, but also to assert national prestige and influence through cultural contacts and interactions. A promotional strategy to display a country's cultural achievements in the international arena can be observed in the early *international exhibitions* of the second half of the 19th century: arts and crafts, later technological innovations and industrial products, even exotic forms of culture from the colonies were proudly offered as proof of the richness, prosperity and progress of a nation.

With the expansion of the railway network across Europe and the development of regular transatlantic steamer transportation, cultural export took off as a commercial enterprise, with musicians and visual artists, stage stars and entire theater companies, celebrated authors and hopeful beginners on the move, seeking new opportunities and audiences, fame, success and riches. Early forms of artistic *mobility* developed, usually without government support, as commercial endeavors and sometimes with the help of rich private patrons, with more risk, trials and tribulations involved than triumph and glory.

⌘   Apart from commercial tours, private and for pleasure travel and the world exhibitions, *migration* also shaped international cultural contacts. Emigration and exile brought artists of different backgrounds together, made them learn from each other and sometimes work together in editing magazines, running debates, staging performances, creating groups of visual artists and common exhibits. Some European cities exercised a special appeal: London and Paris throughout the whole 19th and 20th centuries; Munich and Vienna at the turn of the century, until the outbreak of the World War One; Zurich during the Great War; Berlin and Prague afterwards, in the 1920s, and Amsterdam in the 1930s...

With the onset of Word War I, artistic talents were once again invoked by the state, for the sake of patriotic propaganda and bellicose agitation beyond borders. Many pacifist, peaceful artists and intellectuals quickly dropped their mantle of cosmopolitanism and became warmongers and chauvinists. Trench warfare split Europe and eliminated most of the communication between warring parties, except through neutral Switzerland—where, in the cafes and cabarets of Zurich, a mixed company of refugees and displaced persons kept arguing and collaborating on publishing and stage projects. Dadaism became their label, a sardonic reaction to mass slaughter of the continent, staged as a bawdy series of acts in Cabaret Voltaire.

Culture as propaganda

In the period between the two world wars, national governments in Europe started supporting some cultural exchanges, seeking to enhance their national prestige and influence abroad.

⌘   The French authorities were especially eager to spread the influence of French culture and used seemingly non-governmental organizations such as Alliance Française and a network of French language secondary schools (les lycées françaises) abroad for that purpose. In the mid 1930's Association française d'action artistique (AFAA) was set up as an intermediary, linked to the French Ministry of Foreign Affairs, and endowed with public funds to spread French arts abroad.

⌘   The communist authorities in Soviet Russia made a skillful use of culture to reduce their international political isolation and create a positive impression of revolutionary transformations. They often invited "progressive" journalists, writers and intellectuals to visit the land of the Soviets, and took them on carefully arranged and closely supervised tours so as to create an idealized impression. This cosmetic reworking of drab realities prompted the American poet Lincoln Steffens to say, after returning from Soviet Russia: "I have seen the future, and it works." Some other foreign visitors were more cautious. Soviet authorities used international exhibitions abroad to erect ambitious pavilions, filling them with their cultural and industrial achievements. They also spread Soviet literature and works of art using the network of allied communist parties and various associations under their control.

⌘   The Fascist regime in Italy and the Nazis in Germany followed the Soviet model of culture deployed for propaganda purposes, both at home and abroad. The common objective of these regimes was to subjugate public life entirely to the cult of the leader and the self-aggrandizing ideology of racial superiority. In practice, this meant a strict control of the cultural infrastructure and also government scrutiny of international cultural communication, allowed and aided only if carefully orchestrated for maximum propagandistic effect. The Venice Biennale, initiated by the municipality as an international arts exhibition in 1895, was one of the early recurrent platforms of international representation, yet in 1931, it was taken over by the Fascist state as it sought to enhance its own prestige, adding a film festival to it in 1932, and a drama festival in 1934.

⌘   In contrast to Venice, the Salzburg Festspiele counted more on an international elite audience than international programming from 1918, and was sustained by the charismatic personality of the director Max Reinhardt for twenty years, despite all the political turmoil in Austria. He immigrated to the USA after Hitler's occupation of Austria in 1938, but could not find his proper place in a theater system driven by commerce (*show business*) instead of a benevolent state and wealthy patrons.

International cultural initiatives and platforms independent of political manipulations, ideological objectives and secret agendas were very rare in the inter-war period. Escalating international conflicts, as in Abyssinia, the civil war in Spain and the Sudeten-crisis instigated international mobilization of artists and intellectuals, prompted gestures of organized solidarity and political engagement well beyond the borders of national states. Even before the beginning of World War II, ideological oppositions and political tensions caused a reduction in international cultural communication, with many of its protagonists killed, persecuted or forced into exile between 1933 and 1945.

World War II and post-war reconstruction

Cultural life was greatly disturbed, if not made completely impossible in many countries during World War II, especially those under Nazi occupation. Civilian mobility and communications were curtailed. Anti-fascist exiles from Germany and later from other countries occupied by the Nazis sought refuge in neutral countries such as Turkey, Sweden, Spain and Portugal, emigrated from Europe if they could, or strived to reach Great Britain, where cultural life was also affected by heavy aerial bombing. Occasionally, there were some cultural activities in concentration and POW camps across Europe, but usually organized by inmates of the same nationality and language for their compatriots. Much of the existing cultural infrastructure was destroyed in military operations all over Europe.

Once the war ended with Allied victory, cultural renewal was initiated with great enthusiasm and much government investment. For the first time, most governments in Europe started looking at culture as a *public* matter, and not as a cause dependent predominantly on private initiative and benevolence. With the systematic commitment of public resources to culture the war wounds were supposedly healed, and the values of peace and understanding reaffirmed. The investment inevitably reflected prevailing political ideas and ideological orientations about the democratization of culture, and the emancipation of broad masses of populace through access to high quality cultural products, facilitated by the welfare state.

The United Nations emerged from the Allied victory as an all-embracing international organization, seeking to safeguard peace and strengthen international collaboration. For that purpose, the UN created the United Nations Educational, Scientific and Cultural Organization (UNESCO) in 1945, as an agency to initiate and coordinate international cooperation in the fields stated, with a headquarter in Paris. The effectiveness of this and other UN related organizations was curtailed by Cold War rivalries and distrust, the particular agendas of great powers, which went against the universalist premises proudly proclaimed by the UNESCO.

⌘ Conceived essentially as a standard-setter and clearing house, this organization enlarged its mandate during the decolonization process in response to calls for operational action from its enlarged constituency, i.e. the developing countries. It has nevertheless maintained a keen interest and active presence in European cultural circles (where the idea of UNESCO actually originated). It played a significant role in the Helsinki Process that led to the establishment of the CSCE (OSCE as from 1992). European actors played a major role in conceiving a series of other important conventions adopted under the auspices of UNESCO for the protection of cultural heritage (1954, 1970, 1972, 1995, 2001 and 2003). The best known and most widely ratified of these is the 1972 *Convention concerning the Protection of the World Cultural and Natural Heritage*. The accompanying *World Heritage List* today includes over 800 properties, of which almost half are located in Europe. The principles and norms embodied in these international instruments provide a recognized template for good practice in the heritage conservation disciplines and are actively invoked by European professionals in their work.

Since the end of World War II, international relations in Europe were marked by the opposition of capitalist and communist countries and the emergence of two military political blocks, North Atlantic Treaty Organization (NATO) and the Warsaw Pact. The Cold War, in which they were locked, limited and politicized cultural communication. The Soviet Red Army imposed communist regimes in the Central and Eastern European countries it had liberated at the end of the war. A *Sovietization* of cultural life ensued, with the nationalization of the whole of the cultural infrastructure, generous subsidies coupled with censorship, along with the imposition of ideological dogmas and obligatory aesthetic principles as well as models on cultural professionals and audiences.

The goal of NATO was to contain the military and political expansion of the USSR, and to prevent further communist takeovers in Europe. The influence of US popular culture grew markedly in Western Europe, especially in film and jazz music, while Communist parties and the numerous organizations affiliated with them popularized Soviet culture and its ideological foundations. To make sure Western European artists and intellectuals would not succumb to the influence of Communism, the CIA funded many bogus foundations to hide a steady flow of grants to magazines, publishers, congresses and symposia, even theater and music tours, and festivals, with the Paris office of the Congress for Cultural Freedom used as a front.

The Council of Europe was established in Strasbourg in 1949, as an *intergovernmental* organization to advance peace and collaboration, including culture and education, amongst European democracies. Communist countries in Central and Eastern Europe could not apply for membership because they were not genuine parliamentary democracies, because ideology overruled law, and human rights were systematically abused. In 1954, the Council of Europe adopted its *European Cultural Convention* that was the first effort to codify cultural cooperation among member states, and to set some standards for the role of governments in this field. In its first years of existence, the Council of Europe worked to consolidate the reconciliation process in Europe, to heal the wounds, and overcome the distrust and resentments left over from the war. Later, its efforts were focused on achieving better mutual understanding and appreciation of different cultures in Europe, to build up their validity and merits in the eyes of others through international cultural cooperation. In subsequent decades, the Council of Europe developed its methods and forms of cultural engagement, from large exhibitions on major European cultural-historical themes to "cultural routes", interconnecting heritage sites and monuments. Since most member states kept developing their own cultural systems, it was logical that the Council became a platform to compare approaches and instruments, ultimately to evaluate them and seek more coherence and common points so as to further cooperation among national cultural systems and their protagonists.

⌘   Such cultural interactions were not limited however to the governments and intergovernmental bodies and their initiatives. The PEN Club, founded in 1921 as an independent international organization of writers to affirm the culture of peace and collaboration and defend the freedom of artistic expression through its national chapters and international congresses, was renewed after the war. The Swiss philosopher Denis de Rougemont was the initiator of the European Festival Association (EFA), set up in 1952 as a platform for common reflection and collaboration among the few European international festivals of music and performing arts that appeared after World War Two. There were only a handful of them, in comparison with the thousands today, but even then there was mention of a *festival explosion*.

⌘   With De Rougemont's engagement the European Cultural Foundation was set up in Geneva in 1954, but because it had difficulty ensuring proper funds there, its Chairman at the time, prince Bernhard of the Netherlands, moved it to Amsterdam in 1958 and secured a steady subsidy from a Dutch lottery. The Foundation undertook to finance research projects and artistic work, and also spun off several initiatives such as a cluster of related institutes that in time became independent, as well as early academic mobility schemes.

A great effort to achieve reconciliation and erase the negative traces of previous confrontations and hatred marked post-war French–German relationship. It was an effort led by the post-war governments, but included the engagement of numerous academic and cultural resources, political organizations and movements. With remarkable success history teachers rewrote the text book chapters about the common past, students spent vacations across the border, trade unions swapped activists and cultural exchanges at all levels completed the effort. This process was part of a gradual, small-scale peace building effort in Europe, that also promoted the *twinning* of cities and various youth and student exchange schemes, which gave at least some citizens a chance to learn about their neighbors and fellow Europeans even before the explosion of mass tourism.

Cold War restraints

Other private initiatives of merit, such as numerous learned and artistic societies, conferences, platforms and informal networks were set up to further cultural dialogue in Europe, but they were practically all inhibited by Cold War circumstances, in the sense that usually they only involved individuals and organizations from Western Europe. If, exceptionally, some Eastern European representatives were invited, they were rarely allowed by their own governments to attend, and were replaced by regime loyalists in most instances, who were expected to tow the official line and thus provoked distrust from most of their Western interlocutors.

Cultural programs across the Iron Curtain were rare, and were undertaken to enhance the prestige of the originating country and as a show of good will towards the host country, which in turn reciprocated by accepting the role of host. Such programs were as a rule initiated, stage managed, financed and supervised by governments, and loaded with official and protocol details, and significance.

⌘   A performance of Shakespeare's *Hamlet*, directed by Peter Brook, sent from London to Moscow in 1955, was attended by officials and diplomats and hardly any normal public.

⌘   The guest appearance of Brecht's Berliner Ensemble at the Theater of the Nations festival in Paris a year earlier, was also stage managed by the DDR authorities to gain maximum propagandistic mileage, but unexpectedly left a lasting impression on some French theater artists and experts.

⌘   Rare appearances of Soviet classical ballet companies in the West took place under the close surveillance of the Soviet secret service, anxious that some star dancers might seek to stay in the

West and thus embarrass the regime—as Nureyev, and later Baryshnikov actually did.

Communist countries developed a dense net of cultural relations among themselves, through mutual programs, official tours and visiting delegations, and distributed each other's cultural products, such as films, music and literature in well subsidized translations. Since governments controlled all means of cultural production and distribution, it was not difficult to arrange the intensive flows within heavily subsidized cultural systems, regardless of public interest. Writers' colonies, dachas, sanatoria, congresses and symposia, exhibits and festivals provided ample platforms for artists and cultural functionaries of Central and Eastern Europe to travel and meet each other, and even if they were all carefully selected and watched, and expected to behave in a very official way, they inevitably developed some more personal ties and exchanged views beyond the official agenda and ideological orthodoxy.

Even among Western European countries, cultural ties were mostly arranged in an official manner: performances and concerts with national anthems, diplomats and state functionaries in attendance in the first row, theater tours with official banquets and ambassadorial receptions, flags and speeches, pomp and circumstance marked the international exchange of culture, which was treated as something important and valuable also because it was exceptional, almost rare, and certainly prestigious in terms of its active participants and primarily elite audience.

While most governments posted cultural attachés in their key embassies abroad, bigger and wealthier European countries established specialized agencies to enhance their cultural influence and to strengthen their political impact and prestige internationally through cultural activities. The British Council, Goethe Institute, French cultural centers emerged as large systems tied to the national ministries of foreign affairs, professionally staffed, well funded and eager to reach public opinion leaders in the host countries, acting as brokers of cultural events such as lectures, concerts, performances, screenings, and frequent cocktail parties. And this was by no means a Western European specialty. The USA has been maintaining its own cultural and information services across Europe, and the Soviets and their allies established their own cultural centers, primarily in Warsaw Pact countries, but later in the West as well. The Swedes, Danes, Finns, Italians and then also the Spaniards (after 1975) followed.

The Cold War had bizarre oscillations of varying intensity. More cultural communication across the Iron Curtain was possible in periods of relaxation, but new political confrontations would always cause a slowdown or temporary stop: Soviet intervention in the Hungarian uprising of 1956, the Warsaw Pact occupation of Czechoslovakia in 1968, the Red Army's incursion into Afghanistan in 1979, all had negative cultural consequences, felt across Europe. Numerous points of confrontation of the great super-blocks, such as those around Cuba, South East Asia, the Horn of Africa and Angola created additional tensions. Berlin was a symbolic capital of the Cold War, both an exemplary window of the West in the middle of the DDR, and the capital of the socialist German state with a hammer and circle as its emblem. In 1945, after the war, the city was first divided into four sectors by the occupying allied powers, then to be split in two with a rushed erection of the wall around West Berlin by DDR authorities in the summer of 1961, which meant a complicated regime of access and a constant concentration of tension. Both superpowers used their respective parts of Berlin to display their cultural richness and values, but Berliners themselves were prevented from practically any cultural communication across the wall, and from 1961 until the 1970s they could not even see each other.

Challenges of multiculturalism

The developed countries of Western Europe failed to anticipate the far reaching consequences of their recruitment of "guest workers" from Southern Europe, Turkey and Maghreb in the 1960s. Workers brought in to compensate for domestic labor shortage in times of industrial expansion did not, as expected, go home after a few years, but settled and brought their families over. Two to three generations later, most Western European cities have come to be marked by an altered demography, euphemistically called *multicultural*. Decolonization speeded up this multicultural transformation, especially in Great Britain, France, Portugal, Belgium and the Netherlands, where many people from the former colonies settled just before or immediately after those territories became independent. Illegal emigration, driven by reasons both political and economic, as well as steady floods of refugees from remote zones of conflict and strife further altered the demography of Europe and imposed new sets of challenges on policy makers and ordinary citizens, social care, education, cultural systems and the institutions within those systems.

Cultural communication—both within each country and internationally—gradually lost its homogeneity, and the narrow range of established channels once taken for granted. Numerous *cross-cultural* connections have been made;

new *intercultural* forms and styles have emerged. Immigrants absorbed some traits of the host culture and altered it in the process. But mutual enrichment and transformation have been coupled with tensions, animosity, *cultural distance* and *insecurity*, the painful experience of discrimination, cultural subjugation, exclusion of newcomers and their offspring. Integration came up against some stubborn obstacles and resistance, especially in the numerous urban and peripheral ghettos of poverty, exclusion, unemployment and crime that trapped some immigrants in protracted anger and despair. The process of emancipation of immigrants brought demands for cultural facilities of their own, to be developed so as to nurture *culturally specific* traditions, forms and styles. The emergence of *intercultural platforms* where such distinct cultural resources could interact and create new value has been overly difficult and much delayed.

The explosive development of information and communication technology (the ICT revolution) enhanced communication of all sorts, across Europe and globally. Cultural products became accessible on a variety of digital platforms and cultural industry entered its propulsive phase of globalized production and distribution, overshadowing much of the traditional modes of cultural production and affecting the communication patterns of established cultural institutions with their audiences. In fact, much of traditional public consumption habits have been altered by the broad availability of technologies and cultural products based on it. Films, television, video, CD, DVD, digital cameras and especially the internet have made national borders and demarcations of national cultural systems rather irrelevant. Cultural globalization stimulates diversity and thrives on it, but at the same time, the cultural industry imposes standardization, uniformization, a narrow range of popular codes perpetuated through hits, bestsellers and hype, created by publicity campaigns and clever marketing.

European Union as a cultural factor

The European Union gradually became the dominant force in Europe, determining the economic and the political character of the better part of the continent and affecting to a great extent the life of hundreds of million of citizens. Originating as a Commission for Coal and Steel, for a long time this body did not address cultural issues at all, since they were seen as the exclusive prerogative of national governments at the time. Still, in the mid 1970s, the first voices emerged advocating multilateral cultural cooperation among the member states; in 1972 the ministers of culture met informally for the first time; and in 1988, in Berlin, they issued a common declaration of principles, aspirations and solemn promises. But that was still the European Economic Community (EEC), a limited partnership of 6, then 9 and then in 1980s— with the admission of new democracies Spain, Portugal and Greece—only 12 member states. In 1985, the EEC initiated an inter-governmental program of European Cultural Capitals, inspired by the plea of actress Melina Mercouri, Greek Minister of Culture at the time. Florence, Amsterdam, Berlin, Paris, Glasgow and many other cities followed Athens in arranging a more or less ambitious year-round cultural program of international character, seeking to emanate a diffuse, but presumed spirit of European culture.

In the 1980s, the European Commission became increasingly sympathetic to the notion and practices of international networks in various fields, seeking to organize a policy input of European stakeholders, parallel to member state governments' interests through them. Then in 1989, the sudden and unex-pected collapse of socialism in Eastern and Central Europe, prompted by the *glasnost* and *perestroika* policy of Soviet leader Gorbachev, which was fol-lowed by the rapid disintegration of the Soviet Union, marked the end of the Cold War. The disappearance of hard ideological divisions in Europe gave the European Community a new impetus and in its Maastricht Treaty (1992) it envisaged itself as an unencumbered common market of services, goods, capi-tal and labor, based on a common currency, but also projected itself as an emerging political union that would expand so as to include the post-communist countries among its members and in due time develop a common foreign and security policy. The treaty contained a new article (128, later re-named 151) about European competence in culture that provides the legal basis for later European Commission programs and actions. Those provisions came about with much resistance on the part of some national governments and other opponents in the course of complicated negotiations, with a minis-cule budget coupled with heavy-handed objectives and formal requirements.

Post-communist "transition"

In the years after the end of the Cold War, the post-communist countries of Central and Eastern Europe abolished their formal and informal censorship but did not radically alter the inherited cultural system, marked by many rather heavy and inflexible cultural institutions. In the ensuing rapid socio-economic and political changes many of those institutions became increas-ingly disoriented and passive, or opted for commercial activities to compensate for reductions in public subsidies. Parallelly there has been an explosion of new cultural initiatives in the form of small organizations, festivals, centers, venues, labs, studios, and galleries that made a major contribution to the diversity of the cultural scene, and as a rule, had a pronounced international orientation. This alternative, additional part of the cultural infrastructure could count on hardly any public support (traditionally geared to institutional financing and not to project funding), but was boosted between 1989 and 2003 through the philanthropic engagement of the US billionaire George Soros and his network of Open Society foundations and programs.

⌘   Believing that autonomous cultural initiatives would contribute to the emerging civil society, the Soros foundations supported projects, individual and group mobility, training, and international cooperation, building competencies, professional know-how and complex networks of cultural operators along the way. Culture that was critical, alternative, youth-oriented and cyber emerged, to a great extent thanks to this private intervention, and was set not only on the East-West, but also on the East-East axis, stimulating cooperation within the region. Soros himself, however, resented the emerging dependencies and regular clients, so around 2000 he started reducing and gradually "sun-setting" his foundations, budgets and programs, claiming that those countries about to enter the EU should have become normalized, and therefore did not need his largesse any longer. However, public resources for international cultural cooperation among the countries entering the EU remained very limited (except for the occasional big splash, a representative programs abroad) and no alternative philanthropic partner, no foundation (domestic or foreign) has taken the place of the Soros foundations. OSI is still active in some Balkan countries and outside Europe, but Soros' rushed disengagement left a gap in Central and Eastern Europe that still hurts. Some of his former clients stepped over into the commercial realm in order to survive, or gave up and disappeared altogether.

International organizations and networks

With the introduction of parliamentary democracy and a market economy the former communist countries of Central and Eastern Europe qualified for membership in the Council of Europe, and were all gradually accepted, including the successor states of the former Yugoslavia and the former USSR. Throughout the 1990s the Council became quite engaged in building competences, inspiring modernization of cultural systems and in the systematic evaluation of national cultural policies, seeking common threads, synergies and shared grounds in order to further cultural cooperation. Yet, with EU plans for enlargement by incorporation of 10 new member states, all former communist countries plus Cyprus and Malta (with Bulgaria and Romania required to wait until 2007 and Croatia, Turkey and Macedonia let into the symbolic waiting room in 2005), the EU took over primacy from the Council of Europe in setting the terms for international cultural cooperation, despite its somewhat restricted competence and capacity. In turn, the Council, despite its unique inclusiveness (48 member states) lost some impetus, means and influence.

⌘   The Council of Europe supported the emergence of various international cultural networks and set up a Forum of Cultural Networks in the early 1990s, under its auspices. The Forum was convoked once a year to explore common issues in the growth of networking practices on an international scale. Seeking a truly independent position and more dialogue with the European Union, in 1992, several networks initiated the funding of the European Forum for the Arts and Heritage (EFAH) as a broad platform of debate on European cultural policy issues and as advocate of a cultural dimension of European integration. EFAH developed into an engaged advocate of European cultural policy, pleading for the full implementation of the cultural article of the EU Treaty (including its consolidated paragraph 151:4 in the Treaty of Nice), ampler funds for multilateral cultural cooperation in the EU budget and programs better tailored to the needs of cultural operators. At the same time, EFAH has sought to make those cultural operators understand the EU institutional mechanisms and processes better and has been monitoring, analyzing and seeking to influence decision making concerning cultural cooperation within EU institutions. In this work EFAH could rely on numerous international cultural networks developed in the 1980s and 1990s, such as CIRCLE and ENCATC, encompassing cultural policy researchers and cultural management trainers respectively.

⌘   The European Cultural Foundation turned decisively towards Central and Eastern Europe after the end of the Cold War, and because of the experience it had with the EU Erasmus program for student mobility, it made a contribution to the development and setting up of the EU Tempus program for academic cooperation with post-communist countries. Rather than just give grants for nice project proposals, the Foundation launched several ambitious cultural and artistic programs in Central and Eastern Europe, and with EU enlargement approaching, it sought to make sure that the new expanded EU borders would not cut across established cultural relations of proximity within Eastern and South-Eastern Europe and cause new exclusions and isolation. Since 2000, the Foundation has profiled itself as a strong advocate of European cultural policies that aim to further international cooperation and reduce the disproportion between big and small, rich and poor countries in Europe, as well as between the old, new and future members of the EU.

Cultural consequences of globalization

At the end of the second millennium, the discourse on international cultural cooperation in Europe has surpassed the long standing East-West dichotomies and become dominated by considerations regarding economic globalization and its cultural consequences. International cultural cooperation, as traditionally pursued by governments and carried out by non-commercial cultural operators, has become overshadowed by the rapidly rising cultural industry whose mass-produced digital products, their spin-offs and merchandising flood the markets and appeal to consumers, regardless of national borders. France was the pioneer among the EU countries in supporting its own cultural industry with subsidies, seeking to prop it up against international competition and especially US oligopolies. Gradually, France led the EU to articulate its own programs in support of the film industry, in script development, production and distribution. The neo-liberal conviction that any government subsidy destroys free commercial competition put this regime into some jeopardy, especially in view of the subsequent rounds of liberalization in the World Trade Organization, increasingly open multiple economic sectors for unrestricted competition in trade of goods and services. In the late 1990s France put a brake on the WTO-initiated 'Mutual Investment Agreement' whose effect would have practically been to outlaw any government subsidies. France increasingly took initiatives after 2000, sometimes seconded by Canada, Australia and a few other countries, in defense of its right to shield and support its own cultural industry.

⌘   For a while France insisted on this *exception culturelle*, giving a special status to cultural goods as not just ordinary products, but as precious carriers of national culture and identity and therefore meriting special status and protection. Lacking any firm legal standing, this notion has been gradually replaced with *cultural diversity*, a concept broad enough to engage diverse interests and concerns about the uniformizing impact of cultural industry, weakened indigenous cultural practices, the fragility of immaterial cultural heritage, etc. The International Network for Cultural Diversity was set up as a broad platform in 1998, and has worked with some national governments to usher a *Universal Declaration on Cultural Diversity* through UNESCO, then to embark on drafting an international *Convention on the Protection and Promotion of the Diversity of Cultural Expressions*, accepted by the UNESCO General Assembly in October 2005 and since then ratified by more than 60 governments.

Following the terrorist attacks of September 11, 2001 in the USA, the European Union became increasingly concerned about its relationships with its southern neighbors, especially in the Southern Mediterranean. Nevertheless, any cultural cooperation with this area remains quite limited, curbed by the censorial impulses and bureaucratic meddling of Arab governments as well as the strict visa regime of EU member states, imposed in order to reduce the terrorist threat and to control migration. As the EU strives, with much difficulty and hesitation, to formulate its own coherent foreign and security policy, many cultural operators call for the affirmation of a strong cultural component. Radicalization of Islam, reinforced by the second Palestinian *intifada*, the US lead attack on the Taliban regime in Afghanistan and the invasion of Iraq with its protracted chain of violence foregrounded risks of conflict rather than benefits of cooperation in much of Europe's relationships with its Mediterranean neighbors. The anti-Western rhetoric and political militancy of radical Islam and its implication in terrorism shrink the space for cultural cooperation. Security obsessions in Europe, growing Islamophobia and fundamentalist secularism provide additional brakes. The escalation of religious animosities, cultural differences and political oppositions could also be seen as reasons for more and not less cultural cooperation, but in fact productive opportunities, funds and good will have been fading and courageous operators marginalized and intimidated.

A crowded field of players

If in the first few decades after World War II international cultural cooperation had predominantly been the domain of national governments, their ministries and of diplomacy, this configuration has been dramatically altered in the last 15-20 years. Not only national governments but also many *cities* and *regions* see themselves as autonomous subjects of international cultural cooperation. International organizations, intergovernmental and non-governmental, professional associations and cultural networks, private foundations, consortia, and numerous cultural organizations, initiatives and teams crowd the field and appear in several, not always distinguishable roles—of initiator, operator, manager, coordinator, financier, etc. Among themselves they compete with aspirations, projects and programs—for resources, audiences and media attention. They also have divergent motivations. For some, working internationally means prestige enhancement, for others assertion of own national or regional identity, or a strategy of professional development, or market expansion or consolidation of scarce resources, etc. Political, cultural and increasingly, economic interests are entangled with the artistic ideas and creative engagements. Neither policies and programs nor public and private budgets have been adjusted substantially to follow the explosion of cultural initiatives following the end of the Cold War, this propulsive, dynamic energy that has spilt across Europe and has been turning this once rigidly divided continent into an inclusive, pulsating, polyphonic public space. International cultural cooperation has become, with all its political significance, economic impact and creative achievements, a major trajectory in the construction of a transnational *European citizenship*. Increasingly, cultural operators seek to construct relationships and collaborative projects with partners *outside Europe*, and thus respond to the cultural pressures of economic globalization and draw the contours of a *global citizenship*, the cultural dimension of what Manuel Castells calls the global networking society.

2

CULTURAL REALMS

International cultural cooperation encompasses three distinct realms of culture today: cultural industry, cultural heritage and contemporary arts. Much as those realms are interconnected and interdependent, they have some specific individual features that determine possible cooperative modalities and their impact.

Cultural industry: global oligopolies

Cultural industry covers mass production of cultural goods in an industrial manner, in great quantities and with the application of advanced technology. Even though the origins of the cultural industry go way back to the beginnings of printing in the 15th century, the industrial revolution and steady technological development have enabled the production of huge amounts of goods of extraordinary and consistent quality despite great quantities and at a constantly lowered unit price. After printing, as the dominant form of cultural industry, image, film and sound enlarged the range of products. The revolution in information and communication technology ushered in a broad range of digital formats, interconnected platforms and a synthesis of text, sound and image in constantly altered variants and combinations. Enhanced quality, mass accessibility and a global outreach came with a dramatically improved operational speed and lowered price.

Cultural industry depends on a steady input of creativity from many artists, and on the creativity of software developers and designers for product formation, as well as of many marketing and advertising experts who create needs, new modes of usage, habits, fashions, styles, fads and hype. Many of these diligent and creative individuals are driven by their own desire to innovate, to create something original or stunning. However, the central goal of corporate endeavor is *maximization of profit*. Capital formation, pools of talent and expertise, production capacities, distribution and marketing are organized mostly across national borders and in a dizzying array of cooperative arrangements, partnerships, subcontracting deals, subsidiaries and mutual shareholding relationships along the supply and distribution chains. The entire cultural industry has become globalized. In order to take full advantage of the economy of scale it enforces uniformization and standardization of products, formats, styles and content patterns, and seeks to achieve maximum profits by producing hits and bestsellers, then repeating the success formulae again and again. Producers seek to exploit the habits and preferences of an already captive public through the production of series, offering steady upgrades and titillating their audience with sequels, hoping at the same time to tap additional target groups and hit some previously unexploited niches. Uniformization goes well across cultural differences, diverse languages, differences in life styles and living standard levels in the world, since marketing strategies tend to be adjusted to the local markets.

Today's cultural industry connects players from across the globe. They have been organized primarily in several dominant global conglomerates, which have evolved into veritable oligopolies of tremendous power and impact. They are not all of them North American, but also Japanese and European. One could—with some naiveté or goodwill—call this dynamic industry an example of international cultural cooperation, but trading and venture investment are more appropriate categories under which to describe it. The great array of cultural goods produced includes copies of high quality art works (literature, music, film, visual arts), much of leisure and entertainment, products for instantaneous gratification (games) and of superb educational value (learning software), objects useful for status, prestige and utilitarian applications (fashion). The oligopolies are capable of connecting many of these goods whether it concerns content, style, title, stardom, and can engage in cross marketing and inventive merchandising to boost hype and assert an emerging hit. Moreover, the same oligopolies encompass research, development, production, marketing, distribution and reception, so they can praise, promote, advertise and comment upon the same products in a variety of outlets they themselves own or control, weakening or even eliminating the boundaries between information, advertising and criticism.

Bertelsmann or AOL Time Warner cluster great many companies with tremendous production, distribution and marketing capacity. Microsoft, Google and increasingly Skype, not only set communication patterns, but also modes of research, creativity and cooperation. Nokia and other producers of mobile phones and such fashionable gadgets as Ipod and Blackberry constantly broaden consumer content absorption capacity, prompting consumers to retrieve and exchange cultural goods. IKEA's furniture and household items shape people's everyday living environment, popular fashion brands like H&M, Zara or Mango determine young people's appearance and status, and signal their life style preferences. The iconic readability of much of advertising makes it effective all around the planet, across national, cultural and linguistic borders. MTV and its derivatives impose sound, movement and rhythm patterns on millions of consumers. Endemol's "Big Brother" and other *templates* of entertainment and *reality televison* are multiplied in many national markets. The corporate organization of this kind of cultural production nevertheless rests on the interconnectedness of talent and creativity across the globe, but at the same time leaving it fragmented and anonymous, hidden behind the success of a brand.

Cultural heritage: vulnerable and endangered

Cultural heritage covers both *tangible* and *intangible* cultural heritage. Tangible cultural heritage encompasses archaeological sites, historic monuments and sites, museums, collections, archives and libraries with their holdings. A part of the collections, libraries and architectural monuments is in private possession and not regularly accessible to the public. Intangible cultural heritage covers skills, cultural practices, and forms of cultural memory such as languages and dialects, songs and music, traditional dances, legends, proverbs, rituals, ceremonies, feasts and festivals. Communities have been accumulating, preserving and transforming these artifacts of human creativity throughout the centuries as a resource and a distinct marker of their collective identity. Cultural heritage is a source of collective pride, but often subject to political appropriation, manipulation and hegemonic foregrounding or even repression and willful destruction. Much of material cultural heritage has been disappearing through neglect, unrestricted growth and intensive development, pilfering or as collateral damage in armed conflicts. Objects of cultural heritage have been deliberately effaced to eliminate traces of previous historic existence of specific peoples on some territories, others have been exploited to raise grievances and invoke certain rights, privileges and entitlements. In a globalized world of unsettled, transitory and multiple identities, cultural heritage becomes a privileged marker of continuity, longevity and endurance, a cornerstone of revived or truncated traditions, something precious to posses, claim, then conserve, restore, venerate—and to make money out of, through *cultural tourism.* Tourism itself has been harmful to many cultural heritage sites and monuments not originally intended for the mass invasion of visitors. Reckless commercial interests damage or trivialize cultural heritage through kitschy souvenirs and phony *theme parks* that produce, peddle and exploit *nostalgia.*

International cultural cooperation manifests itself in the joint excavation of archeological sites, in the conservation and restoration of heritage sites, objects and specific collection items, chiefly as a pooling of resources and application of foreign know-how. Another common collaborative mode is inter-museum loans of collection holdings and increasingly nowadays, cooperation of two or more museums from various countries in creating major blockbuster exhibitions. They demand great preparatory work and investment, not just for the composition and arrangement of the exhibit itself, but for the generation of accompanying merchandising that is supposed to help recoup the cost and offer additional exposure to the sponsors. With developments in digital technology, international cooperation has become visible in digital recordings of all the forms of immaterial cultural heritage, especially its most vulnerable aspects, almost condemned to disappearance and oblivion. In the digital storage of objects from museum collections, and especially their image, the monopolistic position of 2-3 major image databases, such as Getty or Microsoft, allows small museums very little leverage, and makes them much less than equal partners in transactions, imposing commercial rather than cooperative terms. Corporate mega-databases have been systematically acquiring the copyright on images from specific museum holdings, and then further exploiting them commercially without allowing museums to profit much from this activity.

An *opposite* of international cultural cooperation in this field, is the systematic stealing of cultural heritage objects, their smuggling and illicit trade, implicating sophisticated and well organized networks in most cases, composed of those who select and command such crimes, those who execute them and those who transport, produce deceitful provenances, engage sellers and find ultimate buyers. International cooperation is a powerful mode of crime prevention and restitution of stolen goods. However, international conventions, specialized police units and international databases of stolen objects have done all together too little to stop or even reduce such practices, affecting mainly small village churches, remote mansions and castles, and small private museums with inadequate security. Dozens of armed conflicts taking place all over the world cause even more damage to cultural heritage and provide additional opportunities for stealing and smuggling.

⌘   A special unit of the Italian *carabinieri* corps has recovered over half a million stolen objects since its inception in 1969.

⌘   The destruction and pilfering of the National Museum, Archive and the National Library in Baghdad at the time of the US military intervention in Iraq, in March 2002, was not prevented by US troops, which had already entered the city. There are even hypotheses that much of the pilfering was commissioned in advance. This scandalous occurrence was later whitewashed by assurances that most stolen art objects were recovered.

⌘   In Europe, much damage to cultural heritage has occurred in armed conflicts: on Cyprus in 1974; in the former Yugoslavia from 1991 to 1995; and again at the time of the NATO intervention in Kosovo in 1999 and in subsequent riots and outbursts of violence there, as in 2004. Churches, fortresses, palaces, theater venues and monuments were willfully destroyed. The burning of the National and University Library in Sarajevo and the destruction of the Old Bridge in Mostar are the most emblematic examples. While some damage was later restored—a new bridge was built in Mostar by engagement of international donors and constructors, another instance of international cultural cooperation—the direct artillery hit on the office building of the Dubrovnik Summer Festival in the fall of 1991 devastated irreparably the photo, poster and news archives of this festival, founded in 1950.

Even in zones spared by war and turmoil, the constant expansion of cities and various infrastructural investments—from building of metro lines to irrigation systems—cause further damage and even destruction of cultural heritage. In 2005, a project to build a dam in Turkey endangered the old Roman baths of Allinaoi. In such cases international cultural cooperation manifests itself as international solidarity in protest, even developing alternative plans that allow the intended infrastructural investment to take place, but without any damage to cultural heritage. International outrage did not, however, prevent the former Taliban regime in Afghanistan from destroying the ancient Buddhist monuments of Bamyan.

The conceptual limitation marking much of cultural heritage and its organized forces (institutions, networks, professional associations, NGO's of friends and supporters) is a traditional *protectionist* and *preservationist* mode of thinking and engagement. There are too few, and only hesitant signals from the field of cultural heritage of wanting to engage in strategic cooperation with the cultural industry and contemporary creativity in order to make cultural heritage more accessible and more effective, especially cultural production, distribution and education. Cultural industry, for instance, is equally capable of producing mass products that pilfer, exploit, distort and trivialize cultural heritage, as it is—if cooperation and know-how are properly stimulated and assured—of developing products that effectively disseminate its values and richness and communicate them to a broad audience, as amply demonstrated by some excellent television series or CD ROMs and DVDs on history and history of arts.

The cooperation of cultural heritage with contemporary creativity is of vital importance if thousands of cultural heritage sites are to acquire a vivid contemporary function as places where art is created (artists' residences, often international ones) or regularly presented. One thinks here of all the cultural heritage sites of Avignon, Spoleto, Rome, Dubrovnik and other old European cities that have provided fascinating platforms for contemporary visual, musical and performing artists to show newly created work and to encounter new audiences. These artists also often work in international teams and ensembles.

⌘   The Portuguese choreographer Rui Horta developed an international center for contemporary dance in Montenor-o-Novo, an adapted former convent in Alentejo that accommodates foreign groups and companies to create new work, and also regularly engages in artistic and educational programming with the population and especially youth in the surrounding towns and villages, where there is very little cultural infrastructure. Nearby, Mertola, an ancient miniscule town of only 3 streets and 1300 inhabitants, but with a clear urban pattern, density and history, faces a dilemma: to become a town-museum, swarmed by daily tourists and gradually taken over by the souvenir merchants, or a town which will make artists feel welcome to settle there to work, to make it viable and alive beyond the tourist season.

Cultural heritage is a highly organized and institutionalized sector, nationally and internationally. Its main challenge today is to pull itself out—much as Baron Von Münchausen did by his own pigtail—of the possessive grip of the nation, national identity and national state and its ideology, to which it has been traditionally subservient in the last 200 years. It is not easy for the cultural heritage sector to adapt itself either to a proactive role in a multicultural society that has arisen from recent waves of intensive migration, and to the globalized world of instantaneous cultural influences, mostly disseminated through industrial means and on various digital platforms. In the perspective of European integration, cultural heritage still needs to assert its European dimension and find ways to contribute—much in association with cultural industry and contemporary creativity—to the emergence of a transnational, European citizenship. Its role in the education of future Europeans and global citizens is undoubtedly a pivotal one.

Contemporary creativity: localized and nomadic

Contemporary art constitutes the most fragile aspect of culture even though both the cultural industry and cultural heritage are heavily dependent on it. The cultural heritage of the future is art being made today. Most contemporary artists cannot survive through market transactions alone and need some sort of private or public support to work. Increasingly they deploy complex technological processes and equipment in their work, which makes it extra costly. For the creation and distribution of their work they are dependent on a great number of *specialized intermediaries*, supporting experts and associates. And yet, despite all these multiple dependencies, most artists jealously cherish their sense of autonomy and follow their own vocation, own predilections, curiosities, techniques and strategies of inspiration and articulation. Some are more communicative and capable of attracting attention to their work than others. Some prefer to work alone, some thrive in artistic teams or are dependent by their very artistic discipline to engage in collective creative processes.

Traditionally, artists are *mobile entrepreneurs* in search of inspiration, training, opportunities, resources, support and audiences. This mobility often means passing through national borders and engaging in collaborative relationships on international scale. During the last fifteen years, mobility has gradually, and somewhat too slowly, become one of the key concepts of cultural policies in Europe. The emergence of an integrated open market in Europe has greatly benefited the mobility of artistic goods. Communication technology has given a major boost to the dissemination of artistic ideas, approaches, practices and arguments. The mobility of artists themselves and of other cultural operators as well, is increasingly seen as a prerequisite for a dynamic cultural climate in Europe, and thus encouraged and supported by a great variety of cultural policy instruments and resources, developed by public authorities on all levels, as well as international bodies, private foundations and cultural operators themselves, under the assumption that it benefits direct participants as well as local cultural operators and their audiences.

⌘   On-The-Move is a special web site, developed as a spin-off from the IETM performing arts network, to offer professionals a wide range of current and essential information on mobility, forthcoming events, working opportunities, funding, legal and social security issues, logistics and finances. It is a constantly updated source, fed by the operators themselves.

Mobility of artists is still inhibited by various national laws and regulations, even within the EU, whose citizens have in principle the right to work and settle anywhere on its territory. In practice, various labor, social and fiscal regulations and professional accreditation requirements, and various benefits regimes are still very much based on the national state frameworks, which in turn are built upon assumptions of a stable, immobile national labor force with full time permanent employment, and are thus ill equipped to deal with mobile, dynamic and often self-employed artists and culture professionals. For professionals coming from outside the EU the obstacles to mobility are even more evident, and have been made even worse recently, because of anti-immigration fears and security precautions. Artists and other cultural operators traveling to work outside the EU for short or long periods are also exposed to bureaucratic barriers, difficult requirements, additional expenses and considerable risk, in the non-EU countries of Europe, and other continents especially. While the international circulation of works of art is, in principle free, or supported by a privileged regime, insurance, indemnities and transport costs sometimes impede ambitions of cooperation.

The mobility of cultural industry products—as overwhelming as it is—does however experience some limitations through a variety of regulations that seek to protect the produce of an individual country or the EU from foreign competition through quotas, customs, taxation or privileged subsidies to national productions and distribution. These contested measures have generated much controversy lately, a whole web of arguments and counter-arguments derived from cultural policy objectives, market liberalization precepts, fiscal considerations, ideological predilections, identity anxieties, all invoked by a baffling range of players: unions and professional associations, governments and international bodies, industry lobbies and cultural networks and other NGOs (Non-Governmental Organizations), the European Commission, the European Parliament, UNESCO and the World Trade Organization (WTO). *Cultural diversity* and *open market* have become ambiguous terms nowadays and function mainly as code words for market protectionism or market dominance, retention of national subsidy regimes or their abolition, competition of the European, North American and increasingly Asian cultural industries, notions of culture as a public good and as national treasures pitted against notions of culture as entertainment and merchandise.

While these battles are still being waged internationally, artists and cultural operators in the non-profit oriented contemporary creative sector tend to side with the altruistic notion of cultural diversity and the treatment of cultural goods as products of a special type, created usually under non-profit circumstances and for non-commercial purpose. They are certainly concerned about the maintenance of the various subsidy regimes and fiscal and social benefits they have traditionally enjoyed in most European countries (although not in the same measure, and not in the same way), especially since the end of World War Two. As their practices evolve simultaneously with a strong local focus and global dynamics and exposure, they are particularly eager to strengthen conditions beneficial to mobility and the elimination of barriers, as well as policies and resources that facilitate international cultural cooperation. Looking at mobility in practice, the following chapters will analyze arguments for international cultural cooperation, its prerequisites, conditions, modes, benefits and associated strategic issues.

3

WHY INTERNATIONAL CULTURAL COOPERATION?

If one were to ask some artists and cultural operators why they work on an international scale and seek international partnerships, they would probably not be quick to mention fame and riches. Rather, a broad range of rather divergent and complex motivations would be voiced. These responses become even more varied if the public authorities and private foundations are questioned about the motives of their support to border crossing cultural cooperation.

Professional development

Individual *artists* and artistic teams and collectives are usually eager to work on an international scale because they expect that international exposure will further their careers, bring them new contacts, professional opportunities and creative stimuli. Some artists also think that this is a good way to compensate for limited opportunities or insufficient exposure in their own home market. There is also something exciting about confronting unknown or unfamiliar circumstances, foreign presenters and producers, a public whose attitudes one cannot guess, and even critics whose reaction is also unpredictable. After repeated experiences, working abroad feels perhaps less adventurous and risky. One gains enough insights to make a comparative analysis of working conditions at home and elsewhere, beyond national borders. In addition, some foreign experiences might be applied at home. Some artists seek to go to specific places abroad more often than to others, or even consider moving to a particular foreign spot for a while, appreciating the advantages of a sophisticated subsidy system, enthusiastic critics, generous patrons, a concerned gallery, or a more developed market available elsewhere. Most artists today assume that international exposure, contacts and collaborative opportunities constitute essential aspects of their careers, reinforce their economic position, provide additional security and bring precious artistic stimuli.

Beyond prestige:
professional and institutional development

Cultural organizations expect that international involvement will make them better known and appreciated abroad, but also that it will endow them with some additional prestige at home, perhaps even strengthening their position within the cultural system, in their immediate environment. Prestige is difficult to pinpoint and measure, and its presumed association with international work comes from the time when engagement across borders was rather rare, almost exceptional and therefore considered automatically important and prestigious. Today, when so many cultural activities have acquired an international dimension, this association is less compelling. Working internationally does not in itself guarantee any special quality or excellence in those involved, and expectations of any automatic prestige boost are no longer so realistic.

Nevertheless, a cultural organization can expect to upgrade its own *professional competence* through international cooperation, learning from the manner in which other cultural organizations operate elsewhere. Comparison, the power of example, innovative solutions, alternative models and practices may all be quite inspiring for both individuals and institutions involved. But even the very best cultural organisation has sufficient reason to work internationally, not only in order to sustain its exemplary role and confirm it again and again, but as a matter of *professional solidarity* as well: by sharing some of its experience and offering its own ingredients of excellence to other peer organizations and individual professionals, thus contributing to the professional development of the field on an international scale.

⌘   After the end of the Cold War many cultural organizations in the West sought new partners in Central and Eastern Europe, but quickly understood that they need to support the development of some competences critical for autonomous operation and international cultural cooperation among their potential partners. Various forms of know-how transfer and training ensued throughout the 1990s, generated on the West-East axis, but not all of it was very efficient, culture-sensitive or appropriate for the circumstances in post-communist countries. The imposition of rigid models and proscribed solutions in ignorance or disregard of markedly different conditions, has caused some understandable irritation and resentment. On the other hand, many cultural operators in post-communist countries have been empowered with new skills and insights, networks have been enlarged and new partnerships have been emerging.

Political interests

National governments initiate, fund and sometimes directly organize international cultural events at home or abroad, seeking to affirm their national culture, to make its achievement better known and more appreciated beyond their borders. Often they see cultural programs as a convenient vehicle to enhance their political standing or influence, or reshape the prevailing, stereotypical or even negative perceptions of their country and to place themselves in a positive, attractive light. Those strivings are labeled *public diplomacy* or *cultural diplomacy* because they seek to create an impact in the public through cultural events. By instigating an ambitious cultural program in a specific country, a government might seek to create a gesture of political allegiance, proximity and friendship, to express its readiness for overall cooperation.

⌘   The Hungarian government organized large-scale programs of Hungarian culture in France, the UK and the Netherlands before and around the time of the enlargement of the European Union in 2004, with the clear ambition of presenting itself as a worthy member state of the EU with a rich, but less known cultural heritage, and a vivid contemporary arts scene. In France, the program was realized with considerable support from the French government that in turn ensured the cooperation of several public institutions. In the UK, the strategy was to use a generous special budget to create an initial critical mass of interest by involving many new partners, in the hope that cooperative engagements between British and Hungarian cultural organizations would be sustained beyond this special season. In the Netherlands, the program was to a large extent built on existing contacts and previous partnerships. The considerable investment made by the Hungarian government had a clear promotional goal. Several other accession states organized similar cultural programs in member states of the EU, to establish their cultural credentials in some way, but also emit a political signal to the countries within the EU they consider their strategic partners. In most cases this sort of government induced programming does not lead to *con-*

tinuing collaborative ties among cultural operators of presenting and host countries, especially after the special budgets made available for the occasion have been spent.

Economic motives

Governments tend to act on *economic* motives as well. If they undertake or support international collaborative programs, besides the hope of generating more appreciation and collaboration, it is also done to bring more artists' commissions, exposure, business, to create clear economic advantages, especially in the disciplines that have a profit potential, such as film, music, design, architecture and fashion. In these efforts governments learn from commercial marketing, and seek to handle their own country and its cultural resources as a single *brand* that could be repositioned and advanced. Support for the international breakthrough of some cultural goods or ideas are expected to bring some short-term or lasting financial benefits.

⌘   The UK for instance, emphasizes its castles, cathedrals, outstanding museums and other aspects of cultural heritage in its tourist publicity, but in its PR geared towards cultural operators internationally, the UK clearly seeks to rid itself of the image of a stuffy, old-fashioned and traditionalist country. In British Council programs and publicity pride of place has been given to *creative industries*, a vague term concocted from a combination of contemporary creativity and cultural industries. This shift from an accent on Shakespeare and Stonehenge to hype design, multimedia, software and fashion seeks to alter traditional perceptions of Great Britain abroad on the one hand, but on the other, also to reinforce the position of the British cultural industry in the globalized market, to position British media, designers, musicians, software developers and their output as innovative market leaders and trendsetters.

Cultural organizations also sometimes engage internationally on grounds of economic needs and expectations. Mostly, they seek to find in the international arena the resources they cannot find at home, to advance their cultural aspirations and projects by connecting with potential partners who have additional means to help realize them. This pooling of resources on a European scale is a necessity for smaller, subsidized, not-for-profit organizations, but also for the commercially oriented cultural organizations, in film production, for instance, where the needed capital cannot be gained from a single source. Co-financing and combined investment are very basic forms of international cultural cooperation in both for-profit and non-profit sectors. To mount a big, blockbuster exhibition of masterpieces may involve considerable investment that no single museum can put together on its own initiative. But three museums might be able to do it jointly and with additional, several months long exposure in 3 cities they might attract a sponsor that none of them could get single-handedly. European museums collaborate often with the foremost US museums on such exhibitions. The financial commitment of several partners, originating in various countries, is also a precondition for financial support from the European Commission through its culture or media programs.

In search of distinction

Increasingly, public authorities in European *cities* and *regions* play an active part in international cultural cooperation, appearing as initiators, facilitators, operators and most frequently, financiers. Cities and regions increasingly see themselves as autonomous players in the international field and conceptualize their role as an extension of their own cultural policy and overall developmental strategy, in conjunction with a range of political, social and economic interests and objectives. Most cities and regions seek to convey their own *specificity*, to articulate their own *distinctiveness*, their special, valuable features, resources and achievements that will distinguish them from all others in their country. Some of them feel that they do not always have to conform to the international cultural policy of their national government, but rather play their own game. Furthermore, they enter into competitive relations with other regions and their own national government in seeking international prominence and visibility, using cultural aspects as a *unique selling point*. For many, international cultural engagement is a way to boost their own *tourist industry* and highlight the cultural side of what they have to offer. For regions with considerable historic tradition and a specific history, and especially if a region is dominated by ethnic and linguistic minorities, international cultural cooperation is a favored trajectory to strengthen a special status of their own territory, to enhance recognition of their specificity abroad, and to create a profile as an autonomous entity, in conjunction with, or rather in contrast to their national state and national government (which may, incidentally, be at any given time run by a different political party).

⌘ Catalonia and the Basque region in Spain as well as Scotland, Wales and Northern Ireland in the UK have been acquiring increasing constitutional and legal prerogatives in the field of culture, which they have applied, among other things, to an active role in international cultural cooperation. Similarly, culture is defined as the prerogative of the federal regions (Länder) in the German Constitution, and a great deal of cultural infrastructure is financed and run by the cities, while the national government has only a decade ago acquired a junior minister in charge of culture and media (*Beauftragte für Kultur und Medien*) within the Federal Chancellery. Cities and regions jealously preserve their cultural prerogatives against the growing ambitions of the German federal government.

⌘ With the federalization of Belgium, all cultural competences, including international cultural cooperation, have been assigned to the Francophone and Dutch speaking communities that more or less overlap with the Walloon and Flemish regions and intersect in the Capital Region of Brussels.

The active role of *municipal governments* in international cultural cooperation—and not only in capital cities and capitals of major regions—reflects the fact that cities are entangled in mutual competition for tourists, investments, jobs, affluent individual and corporate taxpayers, both nationally and internationally. The cultural infrastructure and panoply of international cultural events taking place in a city are seen as indicators of quality of life, as markers of overall climate and of the attractiveness' of a city for creative individuals and dynamic businesses to settle in. City politicians would state that they support international cultural cooperation in order to advance young talent, attract it to the city and to enrich their own audience, especially in the cities of markedly multicultural demography. Here again, cultural, developmental, social, economic and political motives become intermingled.

⌘ Eurocities, a Brussels based network that represents the interests of hundreds of cities towards the institution of the European Union, has also discovered culture as an important field of international cooperation among its members, but chiefly in the function of city marketing and tourist appeal. Les Rencontres, a network of municipal officials for culture, also seeks ways to stimulate international cooperation and disseminate various experiences in revitalizing urban cultures and urban municipal systems, especially in the face of deindustrialization and emergence of large migrant communities.

Despite much effort on the part of many players, not all cultures are equally known and appreciated in the complex European cultural arena, not all cultural operators have equal chances to engage in international cultural cooperation. Bigger and richer countries can secure more exposure and possess more resources than smaller and poorer countries. Individual cultural operators, institutions and representatives of governmental bodies often complain with good reason that their specific cultural richness, talents and achievements lack international visibility and acknowledgment. That is why national governments (and sometimes regional as well!) establish specialized institutions, launch programs and organize large events in order to promote their own culture abroad. They invoke the need to affirm their own *national cultural identity* and some jealously refer to the impact of large *promotional cultural systems* such as the British Council, Goethe Institut network or French cultural centers that are active in hundreds of cities around the world, and often not just in the capitals of foreign countries. Following these examples, governments of some smaller countries have also set up their national cultural centers abroad, at least a few, or as many as they could afford, usually in some major political and cultural capitals, such as Paris or London, or in capitals of neighboring states, or even in some places of special cultural and historic significance.

In recent years, some post-communist countries have established new specialized governmental agencies to promote their national culture internationally (The Latvian Institute in Riga, Adam Mickiewicz Institute in Warsaw) or reorganized existing *quangos* (quasi non-governmental organizations) to carry out such tasks (Romanian Cultural Foundation became the Romanian Cultural Institute and runs, among others, Romanian cultural institutes abroad). Even if they officially state that they exist to further international cultural cooperation, the primary function of these organizations is promotional, their core mission is to stimulate export of their national culture, boost national cultural identity beyond their borders and reinforce it within their diasporic communities.

⌘ *Report on the state of cultural cooperation in Europe,* commissioned by the European Commission from Interarts (Barcelona) and EFAH in 2003, analyzed the strategies and instruments national governments in Europe develop in international cultural cooperation and concluded that most of them have a promotional orientation and seek to achieve political and economic benefits. The approach tends to be bilateral and based on some reciprocity, amounting to *exchange* rather than cooperation.

Exchange is a very rudimentary form of cooperation and amounts in most cases to hardly any cooperation at all; equally, export stimulation usually leads to commercial transactions rather than to cooperation. Seeking to affirm one's own cultural values, talents and achievements internationally is a legitimate goal for individuals, institutions and governments. The cultural consequences of economic globalization and especially the explosive growth of cultural industries, dominated by a few transnational *oligopolies*, have endowed such strivings with greater urgency. There is an unsettling sense that large and rich countries with rich cultural systems and advanced cultural industries set the terms and dominate the market and public attention; and that the cultural output of other countries must conform to these terms and accept a subservient or marginal role. Large scale patterns of migration and the EU integration process have further fuelled anxieties about the future of national identities, national cultures and their specific features. Yet anxieties concerning identity and promotional orientation are not the best drivers of international cultural cooperation. Cooperation processes—that aim to go beyond simple exchange and a reciprocal license to manifest one's own culture across borders—require each party to invest, but also question, modify and further develop their own cultural investment and to create new cultural experiences, values and goods in the course of interaction with others.

Cooperation is about more than promotion

Cultural cooperation encompasses the *exchange* of approaches, models, strategies and policies with the goal of learning from each other's experiences; *pooling of resources, co-financing; technical assistance, transfer of know-how* and *training*; joint *reflection, debate, research* and *experimentation*; and in its most complex forms, cooperation in the creative processes, the *creation* of new artistic works. In all these facets the international component also implies *intercultural* relation and transaction, sometimes even confrontation.

In the following chapters, international cultural cooperation as a promotional activity, initiated primarily in order to boost national prestige, enhance political influence and achieve some economic benefits, will not form the central axis of the argument—much as such engagement may be legitimate and understandable from the point of view of institutions, agencies and governments that undertake it. Rather, the dominant perspective in which international cultural cooperation will be placed is primarily one shaped by the *professional development* of individual and institutional players. Expected benefits and risks will be considered in the first instance, from the viewpoint of those operators who seek ways to grow, advance their professional competence and gather new impulses and inspiration in international cooperation. Often such operators find themselves in a situation where they can work with some partners, and especially agencies and governments, driven by promotional considerations, or willing to invest funds into international projects in expectation of promotional effects. It is important that cultural operators understand that a subsidy giver might well be supporting their work out of different motives from those that are driving them to engage in an international partnership.

Peace, stability and macro-regional cooperation

There is another objective in international cultural cooperation in Europe that transcends the various specific motivations and expectations analyzed so far, and which binds operators and funders, creators, presenters and the public. It is the objective of peace and stability across Europe, built on mutual recognition of cultural differences and specificities, and reinforced by gestures of solidarity and mutual respect. Since the ravages of the World War II culture has been seen as a common good and as a privileged platform for the enhancement of mutual respect, appreciation and trust among people in Europe, despite the ideological divisions of the Cold War. The Helsinki Conference on Security and Stability in Europe confirmed in 1975 the existing political borders within Europe, which had issued from World War Two, but affirmed at the same time the universality of human rights and named culture as a *third pillar* of peace in Europe, next to politics and economy.

Especially since the Cold War ended, international cultural cooperation has been a method of affirming the values of peace, stability and cooperation on the continent. Through cooperative engagement cultural operators advance their knowledge and their understanding of each other, and share it with their *audiences,* who in turn themselves profit from the increased diversity of the cultural offer, its expanded quality and innovation provided by international projects, events and programs. The individual and collective image most

Europeans nurture about their fellow Europeans is still shaped, to a great extent, by mutual *ignorance, prejudice* and *stereotypes*, which international cultural cooperation dispels, overcoming *contentious memories* superimposed by the conflicts, rivalries and injustices of the past. By engaging in international cultural cooperation and sharing its results with the audience, cultural operators are testing and shaping common aspirations and values, thus contributing to the ongoing but contradictory, often halting and stalled process of political and economic *integration* in Europe. Rather than bowing to the pressures of a uniform and homogenized *Euroculture*, feared by many, cultural operators are enhancing the diversity of cultures in Europe and shaping an *integrated, inclusive, polyphonic cultural space* of creativity, reflection, debate and cultural memory. In this emerging cultural space differences are not being effaced, but acknowledged and made understandable and appreciated—which in turn makes the emergence of a Europe-wide *civil society* possible and plausible, superimposed on Europe as an *integrated market,* and on Europe as a complex *political edifice*.

Europe at large, as a zone of cooperation, presupposes intensive *macro-regional* cooperation within Europe (Nordic, Balkan, Danubian countries...) and the immediate neighbors (Mediterranean cooperation). The macro-regional forms of cooperation, which are stimulated by national governments, regional authorities, cities and in some instances by private, civic and international intergovernmental bodies, explore the advantages of physical and cultural proximity, but need to accommodate and hopefully surpass complex and often contentious remembrances of a shared past. Specific political objectives of such cultural cooperation are derived from the fact that political borders among European states rarely match ethnic and linguistic borders.

⌘ Hungarian border regions seek to develop cultural cooperation with the neighboring regions in Slovakia, Romania and Serbia where substantial Hungarian minorities live. Equally, in the Balkans—where national governments often do not see eye to eye—regions belonging to Serbia, Montenegro, Bulgaria, Macedonia, Greece and Albania have been developing international regional cultural cooperation in their proximity, bilaterally and trilaterally. Slovenia has sought to consolidate the cultural life of its minority in the neighboring regions of Austria and Italy, working with the regional authorities of Styria, Carinthia and Friuli-Venezia Gulia and with national governments in Rome and Vienna, respectively.

Metaphorically, politicians often say that ethnic and linguistic minorities create *bridges between the states*. That could be true in principle, but minorities are sometimes used for political manipulation and as pressure of one state upon another. Council of Europe with its standards and norms for minority cultures, OSCE with its monitoring capacity, and increasingly the European Union with its promise of accession, have all contributed to a lessening of tensions caused by minority issues between states, as well as to more cooperation instead of marginalization, or appropriation, and paternalism of minorities and their cultures.

Common language could be a solid base for transborder cooperation, but linguistic proximity sometimes prompts calls for cooperation well beyond macro-regions. Specific languages such as English, French, Spanish, Dutch and Portuguese are used as a base for bilateral and multilateral cultural cooperation within Europe, and in a broader cultural space that includes former colonial possessions. The common origin of Romanic, Germanic, or Slavic languages as a platform for cooperation is rarely invoked nowadays, because these concepts are loaded with a negative historic record and tainted by nationalist and racist ideologies (pangermanism, panslavism). They tend to extrapolate cultural communalities on the basis of shared etymology, rather than explore contemporary differences as a potential resource.

4

FORMS OF COLLABORATION

International cultural cooperation takes place in a rich variety of forms. Some of these forms were introduced a long time ago and have become quite anachronistic today in the much altered political and cultural circumstances in Europe. They have been superseded by more advanced, sophisticated models that rely on the mutual interest of involved parties rather than on any kind of outside prompting and matchmaking. This chapter will describe some of the common *templates* in which cooperative arrangements frequently appear.

Exchange, not cooperation

The most rudimentary form of international cultural cooperation, characteristic of the first decades after World War II and still being practiced today is simple *exchange*.

⌘   A museum lends a traveling exhibition to another museum abroad, and receives temporarily a comparable exhibition in return.

⌘   A theater company comes to a theater company in a foreign city with one or two productions, to play for a couple of evenings, and receives the host company in a visit the next season.

This is rather simple to arrange, the traveling party usually covers travel, the hosting party the costs of stay and there are no fees. At the time when such exchanges were initiated, facilitated and financed by national governments for their own political and promotional reasons the simplicity of the arrangement, its symmetry and built-in reciprocity certainly appealed to the government functionaries who often set the exchange terms in bilateral agreements on cultural cooperation, which they signed with several foreign governments. On basis of the mutual commitments made, they could reserve budgetary means in time, plan and execute projects without much hassle about currency exchange rates and price differences, and without thinking further about the artistic sense and effects. The primary goal at any rate, was to make a political gesture and somewhat enhance national prestige abroad. The danger in this sort of arrangement was, and still is that the cultural organizations nudged by their respective governments into a cooperative relationship actually care little for each other, or that the host party does not have much say in the choice of what it will have to present. Consequently, the artistic effect might disappoint and the resources invested be wasted. This has happened all too often.

Later, in the 1970s and 1980s, some cultural organizations entered into similar exchange arrangements of their own will and choice, relying on their own steady subsidy for costs, or obtaining an extra project subsidy for the exchange project. This is already an advance in relation to government orchestrated exchanges, because it implies a degree of mutual artistic curiosity and affinity between the exchange partners.

Stimulating international curiosity

Today, much of international cooperation takes place outside this exchange model and its constraints of reciprocity, driven by the ambitions of artists and cultural organizations, with the government appearing more in the role of a financier than initiator and arranger. The emergence of a European and global market for the expanding cultural industry also prompted more autonomy and outreach in the actions of the institutional players. Rising international interest in artistic work, and consequently taking it abroad, demands an effective communication strategy to provoke curiosity and find a reliable host partner. Ambitious artists, artistic collectives and cultural organizations deploy a variety of instruments of communication to draw international interest to their activity, such as:

⌘ press releases geared to the international press and especially professional journals,

⌘ multilingual web sites and newsletters,

⌘   active participation in networks,

⌘   invitations, extended to foreign critics, curators and program-mers to attend a specific event or take advantage of a program composed to stimulate their curiosity and appreciation, while

⌘   *show cases,* in the field of performing arts and especially con-temporary dance, give foreign professional visitors a chance to see, over one weekend, a great range of work by various artists and companies made in one country or region.

In some countries these tasks are also carried out by specialized cultural organizations that play a role in the information, documentation and profes-sional development of an artistic discipline and its international profiling, usually with some government support, or by commercially operating *agents* and *impressarios,* especially in the world of music. A small army of *cultural attachés,* working from their embassies, seek to provoke foreign curiosity for their own national culture, and the same task is carried out by hundreds of national cultural centers and institutes abroad, all the outposts of the Goethe Institut, British Council, and their counterparts set up by national govern-ments.

The role of the presenter

In principle, anyone can hire an exhibition hall or a venue in a foreign city for a limited period of time to show their own cultural goods, but there is no sense in investing extensive resources on going abroad with an exhibition, per-formance, concert or documentary film program that no one knows about, and no one is waiting for. A host partner will know better what would make sense, where, and for whom, as well as how to make the local logistical ar-rangements, attract media and public attention. This is also true within one's own country, if one just moves from one city or region to another, but espe-cially abroad, where technical and legal differences in making all necessary arrangements may be more pronounced, and a language barrier may also play a role. Besides, if authors and works are not so well known, *local marketing knowledge* is essential.

An artist, artistic collective or cultural organization might have various mo-tives for going abroad, but success will, to a great extent, depend on the quality of the local host—the *presenter*. The safest way is to seek a strong and competent presenter, obtain his firm commitment to present the foreign work, and then to rely on his motivation and knowledge of local circumstances. A presenter is neither just a hired local troubleshooter, nor a mere fixer, but an *artistic partner*, a programmer with his own idiosyncrasies and predilections, someone who does not take everything offered to him but exercises his own judgment and follows his own taste. Preferably, this is someone who brings in foreign work with some regularity, and therefore enjoys a certain local reputation for quality and appealing choices. The audience trust for the presenter is of critical importance if the body of work to be presented is less known. The presenting organization might have its own venue, concert hall, a gallery or a museum with space for temporary exhibitions, or be capable of arranging the temporary use of such spaces locally.

Presenting work from abroad always involves considerable cost and some risk, and it is better if these are split between the visiting and host party, so as to ensure maximum commitment and involvement on both sides. In commercial culture, shared risks are commensurate with shared earning potential. In non-profit culture, the visiting and host party share in the fundraising effort, they negotiate who will pay which direct expenses and how possible income earned will be split, but also assume the possibility that earnings won't cover costs, and that a regular or project subsidy of one or both parties will be needed to cover the difference. In most cases today, the visiting party will still take care of travel and transportation costs, and the presenter cover local costs and pay out a fee. Of course, the arrangements to be made for a traveling exhibition of visual art or design, a classical music chamber orchestra, a rock group or a small contemporary dance ensemble vary a lot. Negotiations should also specify the technical support to be provided locally, the time needed for preparations, quality of guest accommodations, per diems and the range and intensity of publicity.

The *fee* to be paid depends on the reputation of visiting artists. If this is an individual, a small group or a symphony orchestra, their dependence on subsidy at home in relation to the earned income and the economic power of the presenter (who might also be subsidized) may be a relevant factor. The capacity of the venue determines possible earnings, as well as the local ticket price range, as adjusted to the buying power of inhabitants of the host city, and the popularity of the artistic form presented. Various forms of splitting the box office income, with some minimum guarantee, are also often negotiated.

In many European cities a tango program will have more appeal than contemporary dance, classical music will be preferred over contemporary 'art' music. Lesser known artistic forms will attract smaller audiences and will work only in smaller venues, sometimes so small that the ticket earnings are practically negligible. The range of ticket prices for cultural events varies much in Europe—in general, they tend to be higher in Northern and Western Europe than in Southern and Eastern Europe, and higher in big cities than in small towns. Galleries and museums, hosting foreign temporary exhibitions are, with increasing frequency, asked to pay a fee. They themselves could have a free entry policy, at least on some days of the week and at specific times, but normally charge up to 15 euro for a visit, with discount entry price extended to some categories of visitors. A seat of the same quality, for an event of a comparable sort and quality might be ten times more expensive in one European city than in another. These disparities both stimulate and impede international presentation, making it more or less appealing for some artists to appear with their work in certain countries and cities, also creating inequalities and differences in the intensity and regularity of foreign programming.

⌘   The same economic consideration practically excludes some players who are too expensive, because of their inbuilt, steady costs, and favors smaller and less expensive individuals and collectives who have an appealing offer. Hotel Pro Forma (Copenhagen) finds it difficult to arrange for international presentations of its outstanding productions because the Danish artists are quite costly. In contrast, the Lithuanian company Meno Fortas, of the director Eimuntas Nekrosius, makes most of its income through international co-productions and intensive tours throughout Europe, taking advantage of their low operating costs at home in Vilnius.

Tours

Guest appearances abroad are sometimes extended to tours encompassing several stops, in one or several foreign countries.

⌘   A traveling exhibition is prepared for a showing in 3 galleries, in 3 different countries, and the exposure and the interest provoked may bring more interested hosts.

⌘   A Polish theater company plans appearances in several German cities within a ten days long tour.

⌘ A Spanish cellist plays, on the same trip, with orchestras in Stockholm, Malmö and Copenhagen.

Arranging a tour in one or several neighboring countries within a compact period of time could be made easier if an agent with a good knowledge of hosting opportunities in several cities and even in several countries is engaged. Such an agent usually works on commission. Presenters who regularly feature foreign programs may resent it if a work they want to present is also shown in some other city nearby, because they want *exclusivity* in their marketing and in the media. Presenters in proximity usually know each other well, and act as competitors and collaborators, depending on the circumstances. Sometimes they seek exclusivity in the region, sometimes they might contact their foreign colleagues in relative proximity to check whether they would also be interested in the same work. In this way they might be able to reduce some costs, and make the offer more attractive to the visiting artists.

⌘ A Portuguese dance company appearing in the Tanzquartier in Vienna might make the Cankarjev dom in Ljubljana their next stop. If Trafó, in Budapest, considers presenting a French dance company, it will probably check whether Archa Theater in Prague or Tanec Praha would like to join as another host. But an Italian company appearing at DeSingel in Antwerp should not waste time seeking an opportunity to perform in Gent or Brussels since those cities are too close and thus each city in Belgium covers the entire national market. Galleries also seek exclusivity in their national market. Ljubljana Festival seeks exclusivity in a radius of 200 km, which excludes Triest, Graz and Zagreb.

The setback of *protracted tours* is that they exhaust the traveling party, affect the quality of the work, and may cause them to neglect their obligations at home. Especially long tours beyond European borders may sometimes induce much exhaustion and stress. In some instances, protracted tours abroad make subsidy providers at home rather nervous that local audiences will be neglected. This issue has been raised with the Catalan company La Fura dels Baus, much on the road, ignoring the plea of the authorities, and at another moment with the Dutch Dogtroep, engaged in a series of international projects causing prolonged absences from the Netherlands. Tours abroad might as such, boost the prestige of the artists in their home environment, but they also cause some estrangement and perhaps future vulnerability from funders.

The changing function of festivals

There are quite a lot of programmers in Europe who present foreign work and artists with some frequency. Yet in a rather saturated market with ample cultural offerings already, it has become increasingly difficult to provoke enough interest for an unknown artist or work. Presenting, and especially marketing and publicity costs are constantly rising and competition for the leisure time of audiences has become much harsher. The present explosion of festivals, some lasting just one weekend and some going on for a month or two as an extended special season, indicates the awareness of presenters that it is much easier to fundraise and market a whole programming package than each program separately. Several programs, domestic and foreign, are selected, pressed into a festival formula and communicated to funders, sponsors, media and audience as a special opportunity.

In the first decades after World War II, festivals were a rare opportunity to experience high quality artistic work from abroad that would otherwise have been unavailable. Today, with much more mobility, tours, and digital reproduction, festivals have another, less compensatory, less representative, less informative and more stimulating or affirmative function: they signal and encourage new trends, foreground artistic forms, styles and artists, pursue particular thematic interests, cater to specific audience groups and often use foreign work so as to concentrate and release some local artistic, cultural, social energies and urban development initiatives. They re-contextualize foreign work with an aim to provoke a debate, amplify less audible voices and mobilize and bring together various needs, ambitions and agendas, some artistic, some social, but also political, economic, civic or pertaining to urban planning. In this sense, festivals acquire a *developmental* rather than just a programing role and implicate international participants into local issues and disputes.

Politicians tend to support international festivals and even initiate them, with the expectation that they will boost the image of their city, endow it with international prestige and make it more appealing for investment, settlement of new businesses and creative classes, and tourist visits. In fact, the *economic* impact of most festivals is often somewhat exaggerated. With the exception of a few festivals that have, with their unique appeal, turned their city into a privileged tourist destination—Edinburgh, Avignon, Salzburg, Spoleto—most festivals generate modest economic results, and add to the quality of the tourist programs (and thus perhaps make some tourists spend a bit more money and stay longer), rather than attract tourists on their own strength. Much of the spending ascribed to festivals would occur anyhow within the local economy, and any jobs created by a festival are usually of very short duration, especially as festivals increasingly rely on young interns and volunteers.

The *educational* potential of international festivals is on the other hand much underestimated. The international programming of festivals offers unique opportunities to introduce art practices beyond the national cultural canon into the elementary and secondary school curriculum, to probe the dialectics of tradition and innovation and to stimulate the intercultural competence of students. In order to make festivals work for such educational goals, they need to be disassociated from their obsessive tourist targeting, repositioned to benefit local inhabitants, and emancipated from any elitist connotations. It has been proven that festivals can increase collaborative attitudes of local cultural organizations among themselves, but they can also function as a catalyst to mobilize and bring together various cultural, educational, economic and civic forces in a given city to improve the self-perception of citizens, the overall atmosphere and the quality of life.

⌘   LIFT (London International Festival of Theatre) has immersed some of its productions in the peripheral boroughs of London that in the 1980s were considered dangerous, altering the perceptions of theater goers by collaborating intensively with local artistic and civic organizations. LIFT's educational projects involved schools and their students in the course of the entire academic year, and unravelled within the festival itself. LIFT founding directors Rose Fenton and Lucy Neal describe these complex partnerships in their book *The Turning World*.

Some festivals, biennials and similar artistic programs function in the nexus of the arts and the cultural industry. That applies to major film festivals (Venice, Cannes, Moscow, Rotterdam...), the foremost book fairs (Frankfurt, Gotenborg), and international design and architecture representations and trade shows where commercial results stand more in the focus than artistic value. Besides their highly visible public programming, there is a heavily politicized prize allocation game with much influence peddling and high commercial stakes, and also a busy trading and deal making that takes place in the background. In the visual arts, exhibitions such as the pioneering Venice Biennale (established in 1895) have been copied by many cities, and thrive today not so much on their cooperative function but primarily as trendsetting events, bathed in media attention, set to confirm or rearrange individual artistic reputations and increasingly to affirm the authority of their respective curators.

⌘   Art Basel, for instance, going on strong for almost 40 years, brings together over 300 galleries and features some 2000 artists from the 20th and 21st century. It attracts over 55,000 visitors, with many collectors, dealers and gallerists as well as some 1,800 media representatives among them. The event, taking place in June, has its North American spin-off in Miami Beach (FL) in December. Other similar events taking place in 2007 are: Documenta 12, Kassel, Germany; 10th International Istanbul Biennial, Turkey; 9th Lyon Biennial, France; and, outside of Europe: Auckland Triennial, N. Zeeland; Sharjah Biennial, United Arab Emirates; International Biennial of Cuenca, Ecuador; Biennial Montreal, Canada; and Mercosul Biennial, Porto Alegre, Brazil.

Programs with national labels

Despite the rapid proliferation of festivals and a multiplication of various festival formulae, governments still pursue their promotional obsession by initiating, organizing and financing programs of their own culture abroad: days of their national music, weeks of their national ceramics, festivals of their films, months of their visual arts or letters. There is something naïve in the implicit expectation that a citizen of Riga, Sofia, Rome, Madrid and Luxemburg will rush to profit from such programs just because they feature specifically Finnish music, Polish ceramics, Greek documentary films, or French comics. As an exception, Swedish design would perhaps work as a national brand, and there must be a few analogues, attractive cases where the association of some artistic product and a specific country is widespread (analogous to Italian ham and French cheese!), but in most instances a national label in itself has limited appeal for today's culture audiences, especially within Europe, but in the USA as well. Some lesser-known or unknown national labels, attached to a particular artistic discipline, introducing unknown artistic realms from far continents or playing with exoticism, might perhaps work in Europe, but in general, national labeling has succumbed to the leveling effect of globalization. National governments and their cultural promotion agencies are late to acknowledge this shift. The venue and context, thematic presentation and packaging, the appeal of the concrete artist and the nature of the work itself play the central role in determining a potential public who will attend or stay away. Occasionally, international events highlight one country and its culture for political rather than intrinsically cultural reasons, or in some sort of almost automatic sequence.

⌘   The International Book Fair (Buchmesse) in Frankfurt, as the biggest book trade event, chooses every year to highlight the literature of one specific country. In the past, some countries, such as for instance Hungary in 1999, have been very successful in using this special attention to make their own literature better known and more appreciated, to provide a critical mass of quality translation and accompanying programming, so as to provoke lasting curiosity for their writers and their work. While a few Hungarian authors, such as Konrád or Esterházy, have been frequently translated even before Frankfurt *Schwerpunkt* on Hungarian letters, the highlighting brought more authors to the prolonged attention of European publishers. This effort was crowned with the Nobel Prize for Hungarian author Imre Kertész in 2002.

Professional reflection, debate, training and research

Some forms of international cultural cooperation are focused on intensive interaction between, or among international professional partners, and not on immediate public benefit. In the past 15 years, the number of conferences and symposia bringing cultural operators, artists, experts, researchers and critics together has increased in Europe, quite apart from academic gatherings, and in addition to the regular meetings of international professional associations and networks. These gatherings create opportunities for reflection and debate on some specific cultural issues, where a range of diverse national conditions, experiences and achievements are tested in an international perspective that is compared, critically assessed and enriched with additional elements and dimensions. The participants benefit from a broadening of their referential framework, surprising approaches and confrontational opinions. There is a certain *know-how* transfer that is passed on along an intergenerational, as well as along a geographic axis. When they are well themed, structured and organized, these events further the professional development of the participants and their self-awareness respective to the various contexts and systemic restraints in which they and their counterparts operate. Often these encounters and debates lead to joint initiatives and deeper cooperative engagements. In the worst cases, the events miss a clear thematic focus, firm structure, engaging and provocative speakers, sufficient interactivity and a polemic, debating energy; serving chiefly to make the hosts important. In the best cases, with all the success factors matched, such events shape Europe as an integrated public space and a cultural realm that emanates a communality of interests and aspirations despite—or thanks to—the diversity of approaches and experiences. By now it has become normal practice that a conference on local cultural issues includes one or more foreign participants, invited to offer a broader European perspective.

Similarly, there is a visible increase in *training* opportunities for the arts and cultural professionals that are shaped along a marked international perspective. Beside straight academic programs in arts and culture management and cultural policies that include an international component in the curriculum, internships abroad and foreign teaching faculty, numerous short term workshops, stages and seminars, often organized by the cultural and professional institutions rather than the academic ones, seek to advance professional skills and know-how, benefiting from an international composition of both trainers and trainees. These training events seek to compensate for the inadequacies and anachronistic features of the regular educational system for cultural professionals and reflect the rapid change of working conditions and emerging opportunities that are no longer contained within national borders. The impact of national cultural systems, specific professional and training traditions and their discourse are challenged in this context, enriched with additional and often confronting premises and approaches. These international training events enhance the professional development of participants, but also motivate them to enter into international cooperative projects and make them more competent in carrying them out. Festivals, biennials and conferences often add some workshops, seminars and master classes to their programming, and thus expand their international cooperative function.

⌘ Amsterdam Maastricht Summer University, a spin-off of Felix Meritis, European Center for Arts and Science, located in Amsterdam, has been offering a battery of short intensive summer courses for cultural professionals and advanced students since 1990. Courses are compact (3–5 days), unique, highly interactive, and mainly developed in cooperation with several organizations and networks which signal needs, issues and possible lecturers and point out those circuits where the AMSU could market the courses. Many participants from Central and Eastern Europe, from the Caucasus and increasingly from the Southern Mediterranean have taken part in these courses, also because of the support grants from the Dutch Ministry of Foreign Affairs. Sponsorship and fundraising for cultural organizations, international cultural cooperation, international co-production and touring in the performing arts, development and management of autonomous creative spaces have been recurrently featured in the AMSU courses.

⌘ Among training programs, European Diploma in Cultural Project Management, run by the Fondation Marcel Hicter in Brussels has developed a unique, unorthodox approach. Participants stay at their domicile and work place, but gather in May and October for 10 days in one of the regions of Europe, for intensive site seeing of the cultural infrastructure, meetings with colleagues, seminars with guest trainers and lectures by host experts. Simultaneously they work with the pedagogical team on their thesis project, which they complete at home in collaboration (chiefly by e-mail) with an assigned mentor. Finally, the group gathers in June in the European Cultural Center in Delphi, together with the members of the Orientation Board (experienced researchers, trainers and experts) for intensive 5 days of seminars, workshops and presentations of their theses. More than 400 alumni of the program stay in touch with each other via their own Oracle network, and many have reached responsible positions in culture, such as theater leaders, festival programmers, museum directors, and one has become the minister of culture in one of the Baltic countries.

With the implementation of the principles of the Bologna Declaration in the European higher education system, one could expect that there will be more synchronicity in the organization of academic and professional training in arts and culture, and that the enhanced transborder mobility of students and teachers will in itself bring more international accents into the curricula. One of the most palpable benefits of the Bologna Declaration is the introduction of the European Credit Transfer System (ECTS) in higher education, enabling students to acquire the same number of credit points for the same sort and volume of work at various universities, and to apply them towards one degree. With ECTS, there is also a prospect of professionals accumulating their continuous education credits across Europe, from various training providers, all following the same credit system.

Since the end of the Cold War, cultural *research* has also developed its European dimension. Members of the CIRCLE network focus on one issue in their yearly gatherings and map the relevant cultural policy research and solutions in their respective countries. From this network, consortia emerge to conduct comparative, interconnected research in several cities, regions or countries. This is only partially academic, but often pragmatic, applied research that directly benefits the practitioners. Research consortia group academic departments and institutes, professional organizations, networks, public authorities, their agencies and NGOs.

⌘ Under the auspices of the Council of Europe, a Compendium of national cultural policies has been developed to provide researchers and policy makers with standardized sets of data and indicators; made available on internet as www.culturalpolicies.net, it is periodically updated and covers a growing number of countries thanks to the input of national correspondents.

⌘ Culturelink in Zagreb has created a platform of cultural research that goes beyond the borders of Europe in dissemination of research developments via conferences, electronic bulletins and a printed magazine. Similarly, biweekly ACORNS, an e-bulletin of the International Federation of Arts Councils and Culture Agencies (IFACCA) provides an excellent worldwide overview of cultural developments, news, events, debates and research.

⌘ Eurocult 21 (Urban Cultural Profile Exchange Project in the 21st century) was a thematic network, active between 2003 and 2005, financed by the European Commission (Directorate General Research) under its "Environment and sustainable development program—city of tomorrow and cultural heritage." It brought together 19 city authorities, 6 academic and research institutions from 12 European countries and 2 European networks—Eurocities and ENCATC, to examine and compare the municipal cultural policies and develop new approaches and instruments, especially in view of migration, cultural industry and tourism.

Residencies

International residencies are a protracted form of training, with more emphasis on research and development than on direct transfer of know-how. Artists of various backgrounds are usually offered opportunities to work undisturbed and under privileged conditions for a month, or several months, or in some instances a whole year, alongside other international artists. The rationale is that those artists will inspire each other and that they may discover mutual affinities and interests that could eventually lead them to cooperative projects. These sorts of residencies originate in the 19th century artistic colonies that offered peace and creative concentration away from the hustle and bustle of the busy cities where commercial pressures prevailed. Today, many former convents, castles, fortresses, more or less secluded (La Chartreuse near Avignon, Schloss Solitude near Stuttgart, Morisena in a remote Transylvanian village in Romania...) offer such international residency programs, endowed by local governments, foundations and private donors. The cities run such schemes as well, expecting to nourish their own artistic climate by inviting foreign artists in residence.

⌘   In Cold War circumstances West Berlin sought to reduce its isolation in the midst of the former DDR by running such residencies through DAAD (Deutscher Akademischer Austausch Dienst). In time, DAAD grantees became a vital factor of the Berlin cultural scene, created a rich fund of visual arts pieces that remained in the city as a lasting asset, and many of the grantees chose after the end of the residence to settle in Berlin. After 1990 reunification, Berlin remains one of the favorite cities for artists to live in, despite the fact that the municipality is practically bankrupt, and that public spending on culture has been significantly reduced. Availability of cheap working conditions and housing draws artists to Berlin as much as an awareness that they will be immersed in a strong, international artistic milieu.

⌘   Istanbul Garanti Platform Gallery receives its basic financing from the Turkish Garanti bank, but with clever additional fundraising, every year it brings several international artists for 4 month long residencies, enabling them to interact with their Turkish colleagues and thus reduce their relative international isolation. Those residents contribute to the diversity of artistic life in the gigantic city of 15 million whose cultural infrastructure, especially in the contemporary arts, falls short of its size. A protracted stay enabled some of the residents to create works that have been inspired by the city itself and implemented in its urban texture for the 9th Istanbul Biennale in 2005. The residents and the Garanti Platform Gallery as the key interface are turning Istanbul into an attractive artistic destination.

⌘   Following the common US practice, European universities are increasingly appointing *artists in residence* to enrich their campus life and regular curriculum. Seeking to facilitate the interaction of scientists and artists, the Netherlands Institute for Advanced Studies (NIAS) in Wassenaar is also offering artists in residence grants.

Creating together

A more advanced form of residency is one that invites not just several individual artists, but small artistic teams, offering them opportunities to develop new work. This sort of residency, often international in the composition of participants, is especially effective if it can enable a creative team to meet for a few days several times in the course of two-three years, for instance, and engage in a *phased development* of their project. Individual artists are usually engaged in several projects at the same time, participating in various places and all of them in various phases of development; by getting together periodically they bring in what they have done in the meantime, and seek to advance together towards a new phase. In this way, a composer, a librettist and a director, for instance, might jointly develop a new music theater piece. In all probability they need a series of 5-6 meetings, lasting each between a weekend and a week, to complete the work for the production phase.

In another formula, an artistic organization—a venue or cultural center— invites an established group of artists, domestic or foreign, to come for a residency lasting 2 to 6 months, and develop a new work while profiting from the technical and logistic support of the host. While working on their new piece, the artists in residence could perform some of their previous pieces and offer workshops and educational programs, so that their R&D (research and development) engagement runs parallel with their more public engagement. The host seeks ways to make sure that the new piece can be shown in several other places afterwards, and eventually go on an international tour. In this way a residence becomes a conscious investment in the R&D of a carefully chosen group of artists, but with a clear result objective.

⌘ Victoria in Gent is a flexible artistic organization with a more or less steady pool of artists that produces its own productions and tours them intensively across Europe, but it often accommodates invited artists and artistic teams for a longer period of time and offers them flexibility to develop the creative and programming templates that most suit their interests and needs. The organization adjusts its shape and modus operandi in accordance with the guests in residence and various initiatives that come from the local and international context. Victoria artists themselves take up residence in other similar places abroad.

Co-productions

In its most complex form, international cultural cooperation becomes an institutional co-production, where two or more organizations or groups engage in cooperation and create some new work. They commit their artistic talents and ideas, financial and technical resources and their production and communication capacities to make an ambitious exhibition, a new theater piece, or a film possible. Co-production makes sense if driven by the artistic affinities and curiosities of parties involved, a common vision and aspirations. In some instances, it is in fact not much more than a co-financing arrangement, pooling the resources available to the co-producers and reducing the risk by guaranteeing in advance that the new product will have more exposure and some more distribution outlets. Such arrangements are common in the cultural industry where the investment and the risks are on such a scale that hardly any single party can take them all upon itself. In cinematography, co-production is a common arrangement, especially since several producers, by working together, might tap some development, pre-production subsidies from the EU or the Council of Europe. They commonly collaborate with television organizations from several countries. Expensive art books (*coffee table* books) are sometimes developed by several publishers and simultaneously brought out in few language editions.

Co-production could also ensue in some research and development, reflection and debate events, and expanded series of programs. Multilateral co-productions involve even more difficulties and risks than bilateral ones, and a web of complicating variables might be more pronounced: legal, linguistic, cultural, institutional and other differences come more into play, but the learning and the stimulating impact of such arrangements is also bigger, and there are more chances for profiting from the economies of an expanded scale.

Festivals increasingly choose not only to present foreign works made elsewhere, but instead to enter co-production arrangements with other festivals and producing venues in order to make a rare cooperation of individual artists and teams possible, despite their mutual geographic and cultural distance, or in order to enable a specific group of artists to have extraordinary production possibilities at their disposal.

⌘　Janáček's opera *From the House of the Dead*, directed by Patrice Chéreau and conducted by Pierre Boulez, was staged in spring 2007 thanks to a co-production of Festival Aix-en-Province, Wiener Festwochen, Holland Festival, Metropolitan Opera in New York and Teatro alla Scala in Milano.

⌘　Festival della letteratura in Mantova made a partnership in 2002, with The Guardian Hay Festival (Great Britain) and the Internationales Literaturfestival Berlin (Germany), and since 2003 also with the Bjorsonfestivalen Molde og Nesset (Norway), in order to carry out the project *Scritture giovani/Young writers,* aimed to jointly present each year an edition of six young European writers and their first work.

In comparison with such intensive forms of international cooperation, some other types of international cultural events offer—despite their possible specific value—a low cooperation ingredient: international prizes and competitions (especially in dance and music) assert and advance professional reputations and can influence the international careers of individuals, but do not require much real collaborative engagement. Prizes for translation of foreign literature stimulate international curiosity and excellence of both translators and publishers. Several governments and their agencies offer foreign publishers financial support to translate and publish their literature (French, German, Dutch, Hungarian...), especially in smaller and poorer markets, and where there are few quality translators from that language.

5
WHERE AND HOW TO START?

Those who would like to start working internationally often wonder where to start, how to find a point of entry, a way to reach potential partners and, inevitably—funds. Better not to start with worries about money, but first seek to clarify the purpose and set some strategic direction on the basis of aspirations and resources available. If there is a proper strategy, funding could ultimately be secured, but funding itself should not be the primary consideration. Measuring up own aspirations with own resources is the first step:

- What does one want to achieve through international cooperation, what needs, expectations and ambitions are to be fulfilled through such an engagement?

A nice project idea, developed from this orientation and analysis, should be placed within a larger time frame of professional development, seen in connection with other projects to be carried out with or without an international component.

- What resources are available: talent, ideas, time, experience, network?

- What new demands will international engagement impose, what skills and resources will it require?

Thus international cultural cooperation starts with self-examination and self-definition, with a confrontation of aspirations, resources and needs.

A strategic overview

Most beginning operators have one idea or project and invest a tremendous amount of time and energy in advancing it. It is much better to invest in developing a strategy than in advancing a single action that will probably remain just one incident, if it happens at all. Thinking *strategically* means: to define one's own ambitions, interests and resources in relation to the circumstances at home, competitors and potential partners, allies and supporters and their interests and aspirations, as well as in relation to possible partners, funders and intermediaries abroad. One ought to seek to construct a potential *developmental trajectory* on which several projects could follow and reinforce each other, leading to other possible opportunities, along which experience, means, effects could be recycled and prolonged. Thinking ahead could bring efficiency and focus, but admittedly, for a professional just starting out, it could be quite difficult to envisage such a line of development in all its complexity and unforeseen variables. For a cultural organization, even a small and fragile one, thinking in terms of a strategic orientation rather than one or more incidental projects is almost obligatory—otherwise a dissipation of resources and attention will ensue and any effects would be weakened or lost.

Definition of motivations, expectations, and the type of the project, its temporal and geographical scope, and some preliminary profiling of the potential partner sought will all facilitate a search for collaborators, whether individual or institutional. Some flexibility needs to be calculated in, but also some outer limits in terms of time, staff and budget. Desired artistic and cultural effects need to be articulated in conjunction with political factors that offer special opportunities or cause impediments.

⌘   Approaching elections could, in any given country, for instance, bring a slowdown or even block decision making of possible subsidy providers.

⌘   In some countries, where public authorities are slow with decisions on subsidy distribution and delay payment, it is dangerous to plan events for the beginning of a new financial year because the entire budget might be approved only quite a bit later.

⌘   Political turmoil and political shifts could make a country attract more attention suddenly, and thus offer more support for collaborative engagement there, as happened after the presidential election in Ukraine in November 2004, won by the democratic opposition.

⌘   Upon becoming an official candidate for EU admission in 2004, Turkey attracted more focused political attention, but even before this political breakthrough, some internationally oriented Turkish cultural operators reported more response and interest among potential European partners.

Preparatory adjustments

An individual artist might want to work internationally in order to engage with other artists in the creative process or to find foreign intermediaries to present his/her work abroad. Producers and presenters have their own ideas, want to surprise their audiences with some international work, combine artists of different backgrounds or advance their practice through international contacts. A cultural operator should analyze his/her own capacities and aspirations, those of their own colleagues and collaborators, of their own organization, or—if such an organization doesn't exist yet—of their own group, team, collective or an emerging initiative. For a small cultural organization, going international almost always causes new expenses, increases the workload and possibly creates tensions between the projects at home and the international projects. For a fragile organization, habitually *understaffed* and *overworked*, international engagement could be challenging, but the challenge might also turn out to be too much to bear.

In larger cultural organizations working predominantly within a domestic, national territory, there was a tendency to have a separate department for international relations, or at least one staff member specifically charged with international tasks. Despite the positive effects of such specialization and focus, international work was in this arrangement set up as something *apart,* not concerning the organization as a whole and all of its resources. If international engagement is sought in order to revitalize and further strengthen the organization, it is better for it not to be consigned—in the organizational sense—to a ghetto or monopolized by the leadership, but to be articulated as a common interest and commitment of the *entire organization.*

Small or big, an organization needs certain adjustments to be able to work internationally, to re-focus its own attention and curiosity in the way that it can gather information, seek, establish and sustain relations and communicate with them. Knowledge of *foreign languages* is obviously a critical skill, but a degree of *intercultural competence*, a capacity to understand cultural differences, interpret them and overcome them in a practical way is also of crucial importance. There is a need to build some understanding of how the various *national cultural systems* in Europe work, what differentiates them and what political and economic circumstances determine or influence the functioning of cultural systems. Some of those insights are best gained through open discussion with peers, colleagues, partners, through inquiries, mutual visits and candid talks. For everyone in Europe, whether in a member state of the EU or not, an understanding of the *European integration process*, of the EU institutions, the cultural competences defined in article 151 of the EU Treaty and the programs derived from it is also required. To work internationally means that one's own home experiences, the domestic cultural system and prevailing methods cannot be invoked any longer as the only or mandatory reference— one is obliged to consider, analyze and compare the references, markers and signals coming from a broader European cultural sphere.

An organization that considers engaging in international projects must adjust its own planning, since international projects require more planning ahead. Furthermore, it is desirable to expand the operational capacity, which in practice means seeking additional funds and carefully watching the cash flow. Some internal arrangements should be made about the compensation of collaborators for working time abroad, insurance coverage beyond national borders, standards of travel and accommodation, and what out of pocket expenses will be refunded (or not). Continuous contact within one organization between those who are traveling abroad and those who stay at home is as important as a strategy for how to communicate the activities that do not take place at home and thus risk remaining unnoticed to public, funders and one's own peers. If those who work on international projects do not fully share their experiences with their colleagues in the organization, including difficulties and frustrations, they run a risk of being seen by some as spoiled tourists who are having fun abroad while the rest of the organization is sweating away at home.

Orientation, information and analysis

Lack of experience or lack of some preliminary information could be perceived as intimidating or even as insurmountable barriers, but this can easily be overcome within the immediate surroundings practically everywhere, in talks with more experienced colleagues and organizations. They can advise where to look, what is realistic, feasible and practical and what is not. A new fragile artistic initiative should not hesitate to contact more experienced cultural organizations in its own context to ask for advice, connections, tips, and a joint feasibility assessment. The fear of having one's own brilliant idea appropriated and twisted by a mighty institution, a concern often voiced by beginners, should not—even if perhaps justified to some extent—have a paralyzing impact, and drive one into secretiveness. Anyone who does not talk about their own project to many different people will not be able to find a partner, nor to advance the project. By talking, and explaining what you are up to, you will develop the project and articulate it further, and polish the way you present it to others in addition. The reverse might also happen: an individual or a budding artistic initiative cannot get the ears of a self-important, arrogant cultural organization that perhaps has some experience, insight and contacts, but does not want to share them with the newly arriving players and thus ignores their demand for some orientation and advice. Every starting professional can list, with some bitterness, such examples of institutional arrogance, but also instances of professional solidarity and generous support.

⌘   In almost every country in Europe there are specialized agencies or service organizations supporting international cultural relations, linked to the government or working autonomously. The CCPs (Cultural Contact Points) offer information about the EU cultural program. Relais Culture Europe, for instance, functions as the French CCP, but undertakes a range of additional functions, and a similarly broad package of activities marks the Dutch CCP SICA (Service Centre for International Cultural Activities), the British CCP Euclid, The Slovenian CCP SCCA – Centre for Contemporary Arts.

⌘   Foreign embassies, consulates and national cultural centers and institutes abroad (such as Instituto Cervantes, British Council, Goethe Institut) as well as the representatives of the EU can offer further guidance and information.

⌘   Some organizations specialize in enhancing the international dimension of specific sectors or disciplines. Office national de distribution artistique (ONDA) in Paris and Vlaams Theater Instituut in Brussels (VTI) are the key interfaces respectively for French and Flemish performing artists interested in international cooperation.

They have expertise, documentation, contacts and often some extra means to invest in cooperative projects.

⌘   Some municipalities have established well functioning departments of international affairs that act as informal information desks and occasionally provide advice and support to the cultural organizations willing to explore possibilities of opening up to international work and getting access to EU programs. These municipal offices are particularly supportive wherever the local authorities include arts and culture in their international strategy and where they systematically explore EU programs addressing transnational cooperation, such as INTERREG, for instance, based on the leading role of local and regional authorities. In some cases local chambers of commerce can also provide information about EU programs.

The way in which cultural organizations gather and process information about foreign developments has been altered radically in the last ten to twelve years. In the past, aspiring professionals sought information on cultural life abroad in magazines, in specialized yearbooks and guidebooks, and in documentation kept in specialized libraries only. Today, the core information is available to everyone on the *internet*. Who does what, addresses, dates, deadlines, programs—all that only a decade ago looked like some sort of mystical knowledge available only to selected operators, collected and stored in a systematic way in only a few specialized places and often out of date, or available too late if found at all. Not any longer, especially as Google and other powerful search engines select and filter information available on the internet according to finely set parameters. One does not any longer have to trace, in some obscure place, the programming brochure of a music festival or a catalogue of an international biennale exhibition since the basic data, the programming profile and the recent or forthcoming program are easily to be found on the internet, additional information could be downloaded or requested per e-mail, reviews traced on the web sites of professional journals and recent participants and collaborators located for further consultation and tapped for their experiences and impressions.

⌘   Many cultural organizations missed registering this radical change or reacted to it with delay. Always lacking funds and sufficient staff, they postponed the development of their web site or failed to think through properly what they want to communicate. In practice, most cultural organizations have discovered that they need to completely redesign and restructure their web site every few years. In the beginning, most web sites served only the users within the direct environment, and worked as some sort of electronic visiting card or electronic leaflet, or a monthly program. Gradually cultural organizations learned to distinguish between the information they want to make available to their peers and counterparts, to the media, funding sources and potential sponsors, and to the general public. Only afterwards did they start thinking about their international visibility, providing some core information in English. Organizations that attract foreign tourists as audience, such as major museums, felt this imperative first, but organizations that want to work internationally and to enhance their international standing and appeal among similar professional organizations abroad must also convey different vital information to them—in English inevitably, and hopefully in some other languages as well, even if this turns out to be a somewhat costly and time consuming chore.

A number of specialized sites regularly announce forthcoming cultural events, festivals and conferences, competitions and grant schemes, publications and vacancies and a subscription to their electronic news bulletins is usually free and available to anyone interested. Many highlight interesting and more ambitious and unusual international cooperative projects. Others offer reports, evaluations, analytical articles or web logs on such undertakings. On a strictly informational level, the internet has reduced the differences between traditional cultural capitals and the so-called periphery, between the established and the emerging, institutionalized and informal players. Other disparities and inequalities of course do remain, and the novice practitioner had better be aware of them and take them into account while developing strategies for international engagement. Easy internet access to accurate and updated information is a promising starting point, but communication with possible partners, project articulation, development, funding and implementation impose additional demands—of skill, experience, networking and access to funding. A general cultural-political context favorable to international cultural cooperation cannot be assumed everywhere in Europe at all times, especially as many national cultural systems favor institutional partners and offer little or no support to the starting operators.

Here is a very selective list of some key web sites about culture, arts, culture and development, mobility, networking, international activities, forthcoming events, workshops and conferences. Many of them have a regular e-newsletter to which everyone can subscribe for free. More web sites are listed at the end of the book under *Key Players*.

⌘   ArtServis (www.artservis.org) is a web tool for artists, producers, gallerists, curators, cultural managers and administrators, students, professors, social scientists, operating in the field of contemporary arts, developed and maintained by the Center for Contemporary Arts in Ljubljana.

⌘   On-the-Move (www.on-the-move.org) is a web site dedicated to information about international activities, projects and their funding, in the areas of theatre, dance, music and other performing arts disciplines. It is intended for artists and performing arts professionals from the European Union and its surrounding countries.

⌘   Trans Artist (www.transartists.nl) is an independent on-line database for European artists (visual arts, literature, music, film, performing arts, etc.).

⌘   Spectre (www.post.openoffice.de/cgi-bin/mailman/listinfo/spectre) is an open mailing list for media art and culture in Europe. It offers a channel for practical information exchange concerning events, projects and initiatives organized within the field of media culture, and hosts discussions and critical commentary about the development of art, culture and politics in and beyond Europe.

⌘   ArtFactories (www.artfactories.net) is an international platform of resources dedicated to art and cultural centers, which are born out of citizens' artistic initiatives and based on involvement with communities.

⌘   European Film Promotion (www.efp-online.com) is a network of organizations active in the field of promotion and marketing of European cinema.

⌘   Institute of Network Culture (www.networkcultures.org) functions as a framework within which a variety of studies, publications and meetings can be realized, especially in new media and internet art. As indicated by its name, the INC is also active in setting up and maintaining networks.

⌘ Europa Nostra (www.europanostra.org) is a pan-European federation for cultural heritage, the representative platform of over 200 heritage NGOs active throughout Europe. It brings together heritage experts and professionals as well as citizens engaged in heritage preservation, and gives voice to their concerns in national governments, the European Union, Council of Europe and UNESCO.

⌘ Since mid 2006, Lab for Culture operates a compex portal with news, analyses, case studies, policy documents and much useful information on international cultural cooperation, especially geared to the needs of starting and less experienced operators (www. labforculture.org).

Many exciting projects have been realized in the past 15 years by individuals who had no institutional standing but just original ideas and very strong motivation in the beginning. A distinction between genuine collaborative ideas that might be developed into fully fledged projects only if some interested foreign partners are found, and ambitions to present, introduce, market, tour a ready made cultural product abroad should be reiterated. In the first instance, one seeks genuine partners for a joint development. In the second case, one seeks intermediaries, agents, impresarios, presenters, programmers and curators to open new markets to an existing work. In both cases fundraising will be a critical hurdle to be cleared.

Organizational form and legal status

Individual artists depend on a range of intermediaries, experts and institutions in order to realize their projects, present them to the public, and especially to act across borders. Small groups of novice cultural operators may start by advancing their initiative in an informal manner, or by seeking the auspices of an existing cultural institution, or by formalizing their own *legal status* as a separate organization. This could have a for-profit or not-for-profit status, and among the latter an association with members or an operational foundation are the most common models. In some countries it is easier to register such an organization and claim certain fiscal advantages than in others, where the procedures can be tortuous and expensive, encumbered with various conditions and checks.

⌘ In the Netherlands, a short visit to a notary to define the name and the statutes is followed by a visit to the Chamber of Commerce, where a new non-profit organization is entered in a register for a nominal yearly fee. The entire operation takes no more than a few hours and a few hundred euros in expenses. One acquires a legal status, a separation of risks from one's own private liability and a more favorable position for fundraising than an individual or a collective could enjoy. It is no wonder that several international organizations and networks are legally registered in the Netherlands.

⌘ In the post-communist countries of Central and Eastern Europe there was initially, in the 1990s, often no adequate legislation to formalize the status of a not-for-profit cultural organization that did not belong to the state or to a city. To set up an association of citizens meant fulfilling all kinds of difficult requirements and a long wait for an official approval that might never come. Some non-profit oriented cultural activists chose to register their activity as ordinary business, not very different from a pizzeria, but did not worry much about the fiscal consequences because they did not expect ever to make any profit. Others became foundations, and though that sounded a bit pompous—as if they were set up to dispense grant money—it gave them some sort of legal form. Levan Khetaguri experienced difficulties securing a formal status for his activities in the early years of post-Soviet Georgia. He therefore chose to register his Caucasus Foundation in Amsterdam, which made it easier for him to secure Dutch and West European support and in addition strengthened his status at home in Tbilisi.

A legal entity needs to have some statutes, but for a starting organization that can hardly envisage its future development these founding documents better stick to some essentials, and skip much detail in order to allow enough flexibility for all the unexpected twists and shifts. Otherwise, an expensive and cumbersome statute change might be necessary every once in a while. Of course, the mission and the intended field of activites need to be defined along with a governance model and management prerogatives, in accordance with legal requirements. Once these formalities are settled, a search for proper opportunities and partners can start.

6

THE ART OF PARTNERSHIP

There are many ways to find suitable partners for international cultural co-operation and yet the search could turn out to be long, expensive and complicated, since solid and productive partnerships emerge only from successful personal contacts. That means long talks leading to an understanding of each other's work and context, a recognition of common interests and purpose, identification of some complementarity. Matching ambitions and some *parity of resources* enables interlocutors to transform their relationship into a project partnership.

⌘ From a recent, mass-circulated e-mail that shows how *not* to seek partners:
"Dear all: There is a specific call for proposals in the context of (…) which might be really interesting for us to try. It is up to 80% support – the action is limited just for one year. I already heard that many cultural organizations will submit a proposal, but we should also try. (…) We need a minimum of 7 partners from different countries, even better would be to have more, so we show the "real" network character. The deadline is (…). Who of you is interested? Who knows possible partners from his/her country? Greetings, yours (…)"

In this and many similar cases an approach is made to a broad range of individuals and organizations that are only vaguely known to each other. The prospect of obtaining some money from a public or private source with a very short deadline for application prompts this call, but the content of the possible collaboration is vague, weak or non-existent. The proposal is open: anyone seems to be welcome to join the application in order to create an appearance of wide European representation. Whatever will be put together by the deadline will be a bland, fast-food meal, reeking of opportunism. Even if some money is obtained by a miracle, it will be most likely squandered because there is no solid purpose linking all the partners. Every year, in the weeks before the deadline for the submission of applications to the European Union's cultural program, many cultural organizations receive unexpected offers from unknown counterparts from abroad inviting them to join as partners an application for a project financed by the European Commission. This is an opportunistic and unproductive manner of partner recruitment—asking someone to join a ready made application, make a commitment and just sign on the dotted line, which cannot build trust and common vision nor convince anyone of a professional attitude. On the contrary, such approaches disqualify those who make them.

International networks

The most efficient way to seek appropriate partners for international cooperation is to join some of the many active European cultural *networks*. Originally, in the 1980s, networks appeared as innovative and informal platforms in comparison with the traditional *international organizations* affiliated with UNESCO. These established organizations such as ITI (International Theater Institute), OISTAT (Organisation Internationale des Scènografes, Techniciens et Architectes de Théâtre) or ICOM (International Council of Museums) were often more busy with formal rules and mirroring of Cold War animosities than with content and action, but in the circumstances of the Cold War divisions they nevertheless served as a precious platform for professionals to meet and tell each other about their work. National committees however, acted as gate-keepers, as a filter that kept some professionals out and let others in.

Networks, in contrast, opened the doors to all individual and institutional operators and gradually developed an ethos of flexibility, professionalism and solidarity. Some networks became more formal in time: setting up professionally run secretariats; beginning to charge membership fees; registering themselves as legal bodies with statutes, boards and paid executives; structuring their meetings in a tight schedule of working groups and plenary sessions; and instigating many projects with and amongst their members. They justified the eventual loss of spontaneity with some palpable gains in efficiency and better service to their members.

In 1990s many new networks were set up in an enthusiastic exploration of new post-Cold War opportunities and membership became more inclusive, with new members from Central and Eastern Europe joining their West

European colleagues. Network meetings became occasions to exchange information in an informal manner, to reflect on current developments, to overcome one's sense of loneliness and frustration by sharing it with peers, to learn from the mistakes of others instead of repeating them. Debate, learning, transfer of skills, know-how transfer and mutual inspiration and joint anticipation of the future permeate the discourse of networks. E-mail and internet eased and speeded up communication among members and intensified the sense of common interest and continuity of collective attention between the annual or semiannual meetings and yet, the value of meetings enabling direct conversations and debates remains unchallenged. The better networks succeeded in including operators of four different generations, securing in this way both the transfer of know-how and innovative impulses. At the other end, some networks collapsed because they could not balance their *input/output* energy—members expected too much and invested too little. Some established networks created new networks as a *spin-off* to respond to some more specific interests, but also continued functioning themselves.

⌘ IETM (originally Informal European Theatre Meeting) started in 1981, at an informal beach meeting of a handful of people interested in innovative performing arts and international cooperation. They gathered at the Polverigi Festival on the Italian Adriatic coast to discuss their common interests and opportunities, and decided to bring some of their colleagues with similar interests to the subsequent annual meetings. Within only a few years the gatherings, coming together for a weekend, grew explosively to some 300 people. In 1990 IETM established a governance structure and a professional office in Brussels. It spun off several networks: NewOp/NonOp (new music theater and opera forms), ENICPA (European Network of Information Centers for the Performing Arts), EuNETart (European Network of Art Organizations for Children and Young People), Junge Hunde (emerging artists), DBM (contemporary dance in the Mediterranean area) and several co-production consortia such as Seas and Balkan Express (bringing together performing artists from South East Europe). In recent years IETM has expanded its activities beyond the geographic perimeters of Europe, to the Southern Mediterranean and Central and South-East Asia, held meetings in Central Asia, Beijing and Montreal and started the On-the-Move mobility portal.

Network meetings are excellent opportunities to find out what developments and what sort of international cooperation projects are taking place in any single artistic discipline, but also to seek prospective partners. Because of the large and intensive gatherings, one could talk to dozens of individuals in just a few days and test one's own project ideas against their interests and capacities. Caring networks organize special introductory sessions for *newcomers* to orient them, and even appoint experienced colleagues as *buddies* to guide them around the meeting, introduce them to other colleagues, or suggest other people to talk to in relation to their project ideas. In smaller working sessions newcomers can introduce themselves and present their interests and specific projects.

Pursuing the leads

Real work starts only after the return home from a network meeting: to turn at least some of the *contacts* made into *communications*, and if this leads to further mutual interest and trust, to set up a cooperative project. This might take quite a bit of time, even perhaps 2 to 3 years, with additional personal meetings, vague expressions of interest, more exploration, deepened analysis of common purposes and resources and finally a commitment. Organizations need to plan their work well in advance and cannot afford to jump into a new cooperative project before they have completed ongoing ones, and those planned for the immediate future. Often a prospective partner wants to watch the ongoing work of the counterpart for a while, just to be assured of its quality and professionalism. Insecurity about funding in the forthcoming cycle might prevent some organizations from entering a partnership, since it means making a firm commitment. There are also *false starts*, trust one might give a potential partner who for whatever reason does not turn out to be right, disappoints, pulls out or comes with some unacceptable demands. When this happens, the search for a partner must start anew and some time and material resources are inevitably wasted.

Even though in principle, a suitable partner might be found incidentally, in most cases some *systematic search* will be necessary. As efficient as networks might be in providing a high concentration of potential partners in one place for a short time, there are other methods as well. Reading professional literature, especially periodicals, and perusing the internet might turn up interesting leads, but sooner or later they need to be checked through personal contact, in a *face to face* meeting, after some preliminary inquiries and contact. Among possible scenarios is the one where person A sees the work of person B and becomes so enthusiastic about it that he or she intuitively decides that B should be a partner in a future project. Tracing B, establishing contact, communicating for a while and meeting in person follow. Perhaps in a face to face meeting, B as a person leaves a less remarkable impression than B's artistic work. Thus A might feel disappointed, snubbed or ignored by B, or turned off in some other way. The preliminary enthusiasm of one party will rarely lead to the discovery of mutual interest and the development of a common vision. In another scenario, A talks about a project idea to B, who recommends contact with C and D. Mentioning B helps A to establish contact with them, but those leads turn out to be false. Ultimately, by talking to more people, A gets and pursues more leads that finally bring a productive partnership about.

Appreciation of the artistic work of an artist or a company is not enough to embark on a joint project. Beside artistic value that might be obvious or easily recognizable, one needs to test managerial skills, financial sustainability and other aspects determining the overall "quality" of an organization and not simply its capacity for supplying an outstanding performance, especially if this organization has little or no experience of working internationally. Those who do not have opportunities and means to join some network in order to seek international partners, could build up their cooperative capacity by working in smaller cooperative projects locally or regionally, in expectation that their specific work will be recognized and in time, catch the eye of potential foreign partners.

Better known artists and organizations inevitably receive more invitations not only to present their work, but also to engage in international partnerships. Exposure, visibility, credentials, reputation will prompt more parties to approach them with offers, proposals and project ideas. But there is also such a thing as *overexposure*, a sudden reduction in approaches and proposals received, because there is a feeling that this artist or company is "everywhere" in Europe and thus less attractive, less of a discovery. As much as Europe might appear big and un-transparent, professional cultural and artistic circles are rather narrow and intertwined, so that bad reputations get spread around as fast as good ones. Someone who appears as a difficult or unfair partner, incompetent, arrogant, untrustworthy in a collaborative situation, must expect that these traits will become known quickly within professional circles, spread as rumor or warning, and probably cause *damage to reputation.*

Nurturing trust

Whilst finding a partner might appear to be a difficult task, *keeping* a partner is even more difficult. A common vision and an overlapping or complementary interest needs to be nurtured into a relationship based on *trust*. Trust is not a matter of absolute agreement in all matters, but a sense of reliability that partners stimulate in each other. In this sense, trust is built with a shared purpose, strength of commitment, critical judgment and sincerity that the partners are able to project and detect in each other. Subsequently, trust is reinforced by following all the appointments made and signaling problems whenever they appear, treating them seriously but without drama or panic, accepting criticism, displaying flexibility and offering some understanding for the position and difficulties of the other party. A *crisis* in a collaborative project is always a test of trust and of the quality of the partnership. If the partners succeed in resolving the problem and surmount the crisis, they will feel that their mutual trust has been reinforced and strengthened by the experience.

Even though most international cultural cooperation rests on some institutional base, albeit a weak and limited one, partners discover each other and enter into mutual commitment by individuals meeting, exchanging ideas, reaching an agreement and setting up a course of cooperation. They act in the name of the organizations they represent, but the communication, trust, relationship and thus the entire project are deeply *personalized*. The complementarity and synergy cannot exist at the institutional level if they do not also appear on the level of interpersonal relationships. The departure of one person directly involved in a project from an institution, or a change of staff in charge of a specific project might destabilize the project itself and unsettle the other party. The project needs to be re-personalized between the new individuals put in charge. The formal commitments made in the collaborative agreement may be institutional, but the trust on which the project rests and on which its success depends is always of a personal nature. A personnel change therefore demands a repeated build up of trust.

Tensions, disputes and failures

Accordingly, the consequences of a cooperative project are also not just institutional, but deeply personal. Success is an institutional achievement, yet it is shared as a personal satisfaction among those involved. It happens quite often that an international collaborative project ends with mixed or moderate success, but still leaves a certain *bitterness* between partners because their initial expectations of each other have not been fulfilled. Ultimately, they behaved differently or delivered less than was expected, and the working process was encumbered with tensions, disagreements and recurring, irritating differences that proved difficult and time consuming to solve. In the best cases, partners are able to talk about these frustrations *without blaming* each other, and seek to understand what went wrong and why, so as to identify those *structural* differences or differences of *principle* that have made the collaboration difficult and separate them from accidental mistakes and misunderstandings. Occasionally, the grudge or guilt will remain as some prolonged shadow looming over the completed project. In the worst case, tensions can turn into animosity that may reach third parties as well.

Some partnerships break up before the project is completed, because oppositions become unmanageable and differences cannot be reconciled. One side may conclude that pursuing the project further under the tensions and conflicts clearly manifested presents an unacceptable *risk* and therefore decides to terminate the relationship, feeling that by going on the damage would probably be even greater. By withdrawing, a party can cause the collapse of an entire project or only an interruption, and perhaps the necessity to recruit a replacement after which the project can be pursued in a modified form and setup. Partnership breakdown might evolve into a bitter dispute about responsibility, damage, compensation and blame, causing additional bitterness, energy waste and costs.

In the business world there are established and universally accepted *arbitration* bodies to mediate among parties caught in serious differences that they cannot resolve themselves. In the non-profit world, especially in the world of culture and on the international or at least European scale, such instances do not exist. Grudges and disappointments are shared informally with colleagues in order to be better contained, but without much chance of finding a resolution. Unlike the relationship of a citizen and public authorities, there is no *ombudsman* to offer any redress. International networks consider themselves egalitarian, participatory structures of peers standing for the common interests of all members, and do not therefore have formal grievance committees or similar bodies appointed to provide peer arbitration. This would be seen as a potentially divisive step in most networks, and as an unacceptable imposition of authority by some members over others.

In the world of culture, originality and a unique approach and style are the most appreciated features. Even if they serve the ultimate product and make it distinctive in relation to all other similar products, it needs to be recognized that these attitudes and operational characteristics often make international collaboration—and collaboration in general!—quite difficult and tumultuous. It is more than the sheer narcissism of the artistic world or the banal arrogance of institutional power—in the world of non-profit cultural production and distribution everyone seeks to be different from others and this insistence often comes at the cost of a *collaborative attitude.* Any willingness to accept a professional opinion from a third party in a controversy is therefore also limited or absent. At the same time, disputed matters are of such a subtle and intricate nature that they could only be resolved in a legal procedure with the involvement of professional experts, with long court proceedings bringing only much delayed redress. Anyhow, most non-profit cultural organization would not have the time and money to start a court case. In practice, that means that professional disputes and conflicts have to be contained in the *emotional sphere* of the individuals directly involved. Frustrating experiences and lessons drawn, the sense of mistakes and wrong assessments that were made become a part of an individual's professional burden and a professional asset, a *wisdom* acquired in a difficult way and yet hopefully useful in preventing similar experiences in the future. Certainly, to work internationally, individuals and cultural organizations need a critical mass of intercultural competence, developed as a skill, attitude, mentality, strategy and ultimately as a policy. At the same time, continuous international engagement builds up intercultural competence, brings about this subtle fusion of curiosity and experience, critical judgment and flexibility, ambition and understanding that enable one to approach the other and build up a relationship through a creative process, without ignoring and mystifying cultural differences.

7

DEVELOPING A COLLABORATIVE CROSS-BORDER PROJECT

There is a long distance between the project idea and completion of the project. In the course of development and realization the project itself usually undergoes significant modifications in content, approach, scope, partners, budget and time planning. Nevertheless, in order to develop a project on a firm footing, find proper partners and work out the details of partnership with them, and especially in order to find financial support and distribution outlets, it is important to describe the project in a clear and coherent manner, with all its specific features and original points clearly stressed. If the initiator cannot describe his/her own project idea in a concise and arresting manner, it is unlikely that someone else will grasp its value and show interest in it. By explaining one's own project idea repeatedly to others, the initiator practises how to do it better and modifies details along the way, and shapes new arguments and strong points. The key questions one has to pose to oneself are:

- What is the essence of this project?

- What makes it unique and original, distinctive in relation to many other similar projects being realized across Europe?

- Why does it need to be realized as an international cooperation instead of domestic input alone and what specific advantages and qualities are expected from this international dimension?

- At whom is this project primarily aimed and who will benefit from it?

- With what results?

- What are the prevalent attitudes regarding international cultural cooperation and intercultural engagement in the local environment? Are the main stakeholders and funders supportive, indifferent or negative about this course?

Planning

The essential elements about developing and realizing an international cultural project could be found in any standard *project management* manual. Working internationally, however, involves some additional complicating variables and implies a range of additional points of attention:

- a work concentration capable of handling simultaneous developments in several places, overseeing mobility, and coping with the physical distance of collaborators,

- specific sensitivity for cultural differences, and

- a grasp of surprising differences of cultural and legal systems, institutional setups and professional routines.

In conceptualizing a project it is important to safeguard enough flexibility for the input of partners—there would be little motivation for others to join the project if there is no space left for them to take it as a creative opportunity for themselves.

In artistic projects, some *modifications* ensue from the dynamics of the creative process. While those modifications need to be accommodated as much as possible, especially within the time planning and budget, they also need to be kept in check so as not to derail the project, alter its essential character or deliver results that would in fact contradict the terms under which the partnership and financial support were originally secured. Partners need to agree on

- the purpose of their cooperation and its desired outcome and impact,

- the scope of their cooperation,

- distribution of roles and responsibilities, including the financial ones,

- the engagement of other collaborators and associates,

- the sharing of risks.

If partners are working together for the first time, it is worth discussing *how* they will work, inform and consult each other. Even in these times of incessant e-mail flow and mobile phones, geographic distance can cause some weakening of mutual concentration, a slackening of intensity in the partners' communication. Most organizations and most professionals do not engage in just one project at one time, but juggle several simultaneously and therefore precise scheduling and commitment to regular communication needs to be worked out. That individuals like and trust each other is nice, even essential; in order to work smoothly together they need to grasp each other's institutional culture and context as well.

⌘ *Planning* includes an inventory of resources needed (people, equipment, space, funds, time) and how they will be secured; a time frame with distinctive phasing in the realization of the project, from its conceptual development to implementation, exploitation and wrapping up.

How much of resources can be invested in the project depends on the financial means available to the partners and the funding opportunities they can identify and pursue. Most project concepts are developed thanks to existing resources of the initial partners, but for advanced development and full realization they need to do some additional *project fundraising* from a variety of public and private sources that in turn impose a range of divergent conditions, requirements, criteria and deadlines. Consequently, applications submitted for the same project to different potential financiers could vary in detail and emphasis, but they need to be coherent and consistent in their essential elements:

- title and the description of the project, its background and context

- the main partners, participants, collaborators

- objectives and expected impact

- relation with the mission of the organization and its current activities

- approach to the content material and topic, working method applied

- expected audience outreach in the initial presentation and/or further distribution

- time frame, phasing and an optimal budget

- communication and marketing strategy

- how will the project be documented and evaluated

- who controls the copyright.

In the planning phase the financial situation might not be clear yet, so it might be opportune to start with a *minimal* and an *optimal budget* projection and set out a *fundraising and financing strategy*, which is an arrangement as to which of the partners will approach which potential financing source, in what sequence and with what expected deadline for a response. On the basis of this inventory it is possible to set a *go/no go date* for the beginning of the realization of the project and a deadline for the determination of the definitive budget after core financing has been secured. Some variables, contributions and elements will in most cases remain uncertain for quite a while, but what is important is that the budget anticipates *all* expenditures to be made, with a comprehensive, precise and accurate description and a clear itemization. A budget should also contain a *contingency reserve* of at least 5% of the whole for unexpected costs and price variations. These days, with euro as a major currency in Europe and most other national currencies rather firmly pegged to it, fluctuations in currency exchange rates are rather small and cannot affect an international project very much. However, if there is an extra European component, this might be a point of attention, especially since the US dollar tends to fluctuate in relation to euro. Similarly, the increasing price of oil has inflated the costs of travel and transport and affected everyone's heating bills, and that includes cultural organizations as well.

Presenting the project

To prepare a comprehensive and convincing *project dossier* usually takes considerable time and energy. Besides the items named above, the dossier should contain the profile and biographical sketches with full credits for all the major participants and a description of the institutional partners involved. Illustrations, charts, references are most welcome. The style of the text should be straightforward, clear, well argued, without hyperboles and exaggerated adjectives. Obnoxious self-promotion usually works counterproductively. Research is needed to identify possible funding sources and understand their specific interests and preferences so that the project description can offer arguments and accents that will correspond to them.

A *communication strategy* is an essential part of the project and needs to be properly outlined in the project dossier. International cooperation projects are realized in various places and have a long developmental path. In order to achieve maximum impact once they are completed, there must be a well-phased emission of messages informing all possibly interested parties on the project's inception, development and finally forthcoming time period of presentation or distribution. Possible partners, colleagues, financial backers, sponsors, media, distributors and the audiences themselves need to be made curious about the emerging project and informed about its development, inception, completion and the initial reactions. If the project is realized far away from the usual place of operation of one of the partners, the communication strategy needs to bridge this distance as much as possible. A *media echo* is a crucial success factor, and complex projects need attentive explanation in order to be properly understood by the press. The international dimension needs to be highlighted in terms of participants, their synergy and specific contributions they make to the whole. Communication is not an additional chore to be carried out as a side job, but an essential point of attention: without it the project does not exist in the eyes of others, despite the exceptional quality it may reach.

It makes sense to specify in advance how the project's evolution will be *documented*. This is not just a matter of comprehensive financial documentation and the recording of correspondence and communication with and among all the involved parties, but the documentation of the creative process itself: photos, videos, diaries of the participants, web logs, audio recordings are among the possible means to be used. The documentation could be used

- for internal communication and feed back among the partners

- in public communication and promotion before and after the completion of the project

- in relationship with the subsidy providers and sponsors

- for the portfolio buildup of the involved collaborators

- for the dossiers of subsequent projects

- for research and training

- for evaluation of the project by the parties involved.

Evaluation of the project by the partners is an inherent part of the cooperative relationship. In order to be effective, the starting points for evaluation, and the issues and criteria need to be set up in advance. If the partners are in a position to define clear objectives for their cooperation, they should at the very end check whether they have reached those objectives. To do so they would need to define some *criteria* and *quantitative indicators*. The evaluation is focused on the outcome of the project, its achievements and echoes, but needs to include the entire process in order to draw lessons for the next cooperative engagements. A personal sense of satisfaction, problems in the cooperation and communication, and even some small misunderstandings, irritations and disagreements should be discussed sincerely as a normal, human part of the experience. If some major difficulties have occurred, they need to be analyzed in detail, not for the sake of blaming each other, but in order to understand the causes and gain some critical and self-critical insight in the problem solving approaches of the project's participants.

Some prolonged multilateral projects tend to set up a special informal *advisory body* of expert colleagues and friends to follow the project and offer advice and critical feedback along the way, perhaps also to strengthen public relations and visibility. If such a body is established, its members should also have a pre-assigned role in the project evaluation, but in order to fulfill this role they need to be properly and continuously informed.

If the project initiators want to seek sponsorship in addition to public and private funding, another document needs to be prepared, a *sponsorship dossier* that might prompt the companies of a specific profile and type to show interest in acting as sponsors. Before the document can be prepared one must do research and hard thinking on what sort of companies might care to be associated with the project. The dossier can then be specifically geared at them. This dossier should also outline what project producers can offer sponsors in return. Sponsorship is always a *commercial transaction* where a corporation offers some financial means or sponsorship in kind (goods, services) to a cultural project and the producers of the project offer the corporation some exposure within a particular targeted audience group in return, provide visibility, prestige, and a set of associations linked to a corporate product. Even large international companies usually make their sponsorship decisions locally, in accordance with the opportunities of a specific market, so that an international project must seek sponsors in relation to its *local exposure* points rather than its international character.

⌘ An Italian–Spanish co-production, for instance, might take into account the penetration of some Spanish banks into the Italian banking market and thus seek sponsorship for its radiation in Italy from an Italian bank that was recently taken over by a Spanish bank. Perhaps the bank is worth approaching under the hypothesis that it could be eager to secure the good will of Italian clients. In this case, the sponsorship decision would be made by the bankers in Italy, and almost certainly not by those in Spain.

Realization

In professional work it is normal to articulate agreements reached about any cooperative engagement in the form of a *legal contract*. The contract should contain the project definition, description and objectives in the introductory part and then spell out the mutual obligations of the contracting parties, procedures in the case of disagreement or crisis and also some other details. The budget should also be incorporated. It is habitual to define which court should be involved should there be disagreements that escalate all the way into a judicial case. If there are some significant subsequent elements affecting the development and exploitation of the project, they could be formulated in further *appendices*.

Once the project is defined, its budget made and financing secured, collaborators engaged and mutual relationships contractually agreed upon, the implementation can begin. It usually involves hard, intensive work by many collaborators, perhaps divided in several distinct phases and carried out in various teams with their own leadership, resources and planning (artistic team, technical staff, communication, financial backing, logistics, etc.). Not all parts of the team move along the time line at the same speed, some collaborators go ahead of others. Some are anticipating the subsequent phase and are arranging conditions for its realization. Work might run in parallel in two or more different places in different countries. The main executive of the project (the executive producer or however else it is named) supervises the entire process, keeps the budget and secures respect for the time planning. Furthermore, this person has the ultimate responsibility for the quality and punctuality of the work of all teams, monitors the evolution of the project and intervenes to troubleshoot and coordinate between the interdependent teams. Projects of course vary greatly in size, complexity and duration. To co-produce an exhibition in cooperation between 2 or 3 museums, or a biennale, a dance production or an installation in a public space, each demands its own way of work.

Sometimes there is a cluster of various simultaneous projects coming together within the same framework, as in several co-productions of a festival, or like the multiple exhibits, debates and projections that happen within the program of the Venice Biennale. Or there is a festival that contains presentations of selected productions from abroad, a few co-productions, debates, master classes and workshops, some exhibits and a small conference. Each of those might constitute an international cooperative project. The most complex program of this sort is the Cultural Capital of Europe, an official designation by the EU, with a program running in a specific city for 10-11 months and containing hundreds of international cooperative projects, conceived, planned and developed over a period of several years. For example, in 2004, Lille as a Cultural Capital of Europe had at its disposal a hefty sum of euro 72 million and that huge amount generated many international projects. In 2007, Luxemburg as a Cultural Capital of Europe decided to involve all of the Dutchy of Luxemburg and the adjacent regions in Belgium, Germany and France.

The real test of the executive producer is when things start going seriously wrong, when a *crisis* erupts and the continuation of the project is endangered. Those things happen, sometimes on financial or logistical grounds, more often because of the clashes of artistic egos in a team that cannot agree and collaborate properly. Radical decisions may need to be taken under much stress, and taken at once. Consequently, a project might shift gear, be realigned in such a way that some of its essential outlines get altered. There is a need to inform collaborators internally about the changes occurring immediately, and give them a clear sense of the terms under which continuity is assured, but also to communicate the changes to financial supporters and distributors/presenters, and to set up a media strategy—whether by going to the media on own initiative or standing by with a well prepared and coherent story when the media shows an interest, prompted by rumors or incriminating interviews and statements.

Exploitation and distribution

It is not enough simply to create a project—from the very beginning a strategy needs to be developed as to how the completed project will be presented, toured, exploited or distributed, how it will reach its intended audience, under what conditions, where, for how long...?

⌘ An exhibition is made for touring and the places where it will come to be presented are fixed in advance with opening and closing dates, space requirements, a separate communication campaign for each place, accompanying publicity material and merchandising developed and ordered.

⌘ A theater co-production will open in one venue, then be presented in 3 more venues and at 2 festivals in different countries. It is hoped that this will offer sufficient exposure, so some interested presenters will come along, and therefore another period in the following year is reserved as an option for an extended tour, if it happens.

⌘ A new music piece will be developed, premiered in a concert hall, toured to 3 other cities and a CD or a DVD will be recorded at the final place of performance.

The co-producers are working from the beginning to ensure that the project reaches a maximum audience in a most *compressed* period of time and enjoys a prolonged *shelf life* if the exposure and generated income are to meet the cost which will be incurred with the prolongation. Often international cultural projects incur such high costs in the creative process that they cannot be recouped with extended presentation or distribution. Consequently they are only available for a very short time, unless additional fundraising is possible. In international projects, collaborators are assembled from various places and can be re-grouped and kept together for a limited time only, with great scheduling effort. Afterwards, there is little probability that they can get together again, even if there is a strong demand for the product. Therefore some contracts stipulate an option from the beginning to engage protagonists for another series or row of performances at some specified point at a later date if there is sufficient demand to cover the costs. Even if the exploitation of the project comes to an end rather quickly, it is important to wrap up the project with all the documentation, records and copyright issues fully regulated so that it can be renewed if there is sufficient interest and opportunity.

8

POLITICS & PUBLIC FUNDING

In a world divided by borders between national states, international cultural cooperation develops cross-border relationships and products and as a result, inevitably acquires political significance or embodies some political rationale, interests and priorities. This is so even in Europe, despite its advanced degree of economic and political integration and a great range of intergovernmental organizations.

Political context

Most cultural operators insist on their operational *autonomy*, and yet they are also aware of the fact that they operate in a specific political context which they imply or take along whenever they engage in international cooperative projects. Some operators seek to exploit various political opportunities in order to develop their project and watch and analyze political trends to find out what specific engagements may bring them the political good will of the authorities. If their government is encouraging relations with Germany, they will seek German partners. If the government is focused on improving or intensifying its ties with Russia, they will think about finding Russian partners for cooperation. Other, less opportunistic players invent an international project and then strive to enlist political support, hoping that it might translate into some concrete help, facilitation and perhaps even financial means.

There are cultural professionals, however, who prefer to stay at a safe distance from politics, eager to avoid any sort of instrumentalization and appropriation by political bodies, parties and governments; it is a purist stance that can hardly be sustained in reality. At the other pole there are those cultural operators who disregard political circumstances, or even seek to alter them by developing specific international projects with peers from countries with whom their own government has no friendly relations or no relations at all. They consciously go against the stances and attitudes of their own government and conduct, in this sense, their own foreign policy in the form of international cultural cooperation.

⌘ "Leaps of Faith", an artistic project, set in May 2005 on the "green line" in Nicosia, separating the Turkish controlled part of the island from the rest of the Republic of Cyprus, finally overcame the long standing isolation of Turkish Cypriot artists, caught in the tiny realm of the "Turkish Republic of North Cyprus", recognized by Turkey but no one else. After 31 years of separation, Turkish Cypriot and Greek Cypriot artists, as well as those from Turkey and Greece, met in and around the sensitive UN controlled buffer zone in the context of an international exhibit, arranged by a Greek and a Turkish curator. A site specific intervention in the divided urban core was made possible by the recent opening up of the "green line," which prompted many locals and international visitors to cross it.

⌘ This political advance made organizers of Manifesta, an itinerant international and biennial arts exhibit, decide to hold Manifesta 6 in Nicosia, in the form of an arts academy from September to December 2006, as a bicommunal event to take place on both sides of the "green line." Unexpectedly, in June 2006 Nicosia for Arts, a local host, cancelled the program, fired the curators and demanded financial compensation from Manifesta, a non-profit organization with a seat in Amsterdam. Greek Cypriot politicians who initially agreed with Manifesta's terms and plans did not want to allow setting up of cultural infrastructure in a part of the island they see as Turkish occupied territory. The preparatory work was wasted and could not be further developed and realized elsewhere under the threat of court penalties. The long standing political confrontation on the island prevailed over the good will accumulated in an international artistic initiative. A long court case between Nicosia and Manifesta International Foundation is still going on. In the meantime, Manifesta is practically paralyzed, gagged by a court order and with its bank account blocked.

If there are bad political relationships in a region, or no diplomatic ties between two governments, operators from a third country might offer their own facilities as a neutral territory for encounter and cooperation.

⌘   During the war in former Yugoslavia from 1991 to 1995, artists from former Yugoslav republics could not meet easily across the newly drawn national borders of the successor states. If they did meet at all, that happened in neighboring countries, aided by the efforts of third parties, be they Austrian, German, Swedish or French cultural organizations. Similarly, the Caucasus Cultural Foundation in Tbilisi (Georgia) has for years been organizing various conferences, workshops, festivals and cultural fairs that all offered Armenian and Azeri cultural operators, whose countries have been engaged in a protracted and unresolved conflict about the Nagorno Karabakh, a precious opportunity for encounter and discussion. Even if those meetings amounted to less than full-fledged cooperation, they helped keep some channels of communication open, in the hope that cooperation might one day become possible. For the ex-Yugoslavs that has indeed become a reality after 2001.

The relationship between national government authorities and cultural professionals who operate internationally is a complex one. Sometimes authorities informally nudge cultural professionals to engage in a cooperative project that could be seen as a positive political signal from one government to another one. In other instances, a government might react with anger against initiatives for cultural cooperation that it sees as an opposition to its foreign policy tenets, or as an effort to undermine them. Despite an advanced degree of political integration within the EU, including candidate countries and those with some prospect of distant accession, as well as the peace reinforcing engagement of OSCE (Organization for Security and Cooperation in Europe), post Cold-War Europe is not completely free of political tensions and bilateral troubles. The Czech government opposes the reparation claims of some Germans expelled from Czechoslovakia after the end of World War Two; Moldavia is in troubled relations with Russia over Transdniestria, a part of its territory it does not control; the Baltic and Caucasian states that were once part of the former Soviet Union, and especially those with a sizeable Russian minority (such as Estonia and Latvia), have an uneasy relationship with Russia as well. Cyprus, divided and partially occupied, is a prolonged cause of friction between Greece and Turkey. So even in Europe—not to mention the rest of the world, with its multiple and protracted conflicts—international cultural cooperation follows, reflects and challenges some foreign political contingencies and interests, especially when it is quite dependent on the financial assistance of public authorities.

International cultural cooperation probes some of the contentious issues above, compensates for the blockade of political initiatives, symbolizes their successes or seeks to force some political breakthrough in bilateral political relationships between governments.

⌘ Over recent years there have been several international cultural projects aiming to reduce the isolation of cultural life in Kaliningrad, which has remained a separate Russian region after the collapse of the Soviet Union, clinched between Poland and Lithuania and no territorial link to the rest of Russia. With Poland and Lithuania joining the EU in 2004, the limited mobility of the inhabitants of Kaliningrad region has been reduced even more by the EU visa regime.

⌘ The Golden Mask Performing Arts Festival in Moscow decided to organize an edition of its program in Riga and Tallinn in order to compensate for the loss of cultural communication and cooperation that has ensued after the independence of Latvia and Estonia. Regular and intensive cultural traffic with Moscow, normal during Soviet times, was replaced by an icy distancing, disappearance of the public usage of the Russian language and much bickering between Russian and Baltic state governments about the status and rights of their substantial Russian minority. After a 15 year long gap, the Golden Mask initiative seeks to refresh Riga and Tallinn audience awareness about contemporary performing arts in Russia, by appearing in the main venues, aiming at the mainstream public interested in culture, rather than a paternalistic focus on Russian minority audience alone.

Public authorities

Financial support from public authorities for various international cooperation projects almost always comes on political, rather than on purely cultural or artistic grounds, even if engineered through some seemingly neutral distribution mechanism and based on *peer review* rather than on the decision of politicians and civil servants. Nevertheless, in most European countries, cultural operators would consider public authorities as the first and most obvious source of financial support for an international project, because for the greatest part, domestic cultural life also prospers on the basis of a steady government investment.

⌘   Not so in Turkey, where initiators would rather approach foreign embassies and cultural centers of the EU countries or some of the Turkish corporate foundations or commercial sponsors. Most Turkish operators would quickly admit that they expect nothing or very little of their own Ministry of Culture and Tourism whose annual budget of €440 million (2006) goes almost entirely to tourism, and only a few percent is reserved for the support of a small number of state cultural institutions—two dozen repertory ensembles, a few symphony orchestras, 3 or 4 opera companies and some 50 museums.

National governments have developed various financing schemes to support international cultural cooperation through their ministries of culture and foreign affairs or certain specialized QUANGOs (Quasi-Non-Governmental Organizations) and funds. Hungary, Latvia, Estonia, Romania and some other Eastern and Central European countries have created special *para-governmental* funds for project financing of cultural activities, including international ones, based on income from lotteries or part of a tax on drinks, tobacco or sound and image carriers. Procedures, deadlines, criteria, decision-making processes and the frequency of decision taking vary a great deal. Where such applications can be submitted only once or twice a year, cultural operators have less flexibility and need to plan their international engagement well in advance. Paradoxically, in countries where the ministry of culture distributes almost the entire budget to the usual clients, the public institutions of culture that receive their subsidies regardless of the quality and quantity of their output (e.g. Latvia, Romania), newly established national cultural funds for project financing are the only bodies capable of making cultural policy because they have uncommitted means and can spend them on projects, including those with an international dimension.

⌘   Autonomous cultural operators in Romania complain that they cannot use the funds made available for international cultural cooperation by the ministries of Culture and Foreign Affairs and by the Romanian Cultural Institute in 2007, after Romanian accession to the EU, because of the rigid regulations designed by the Ministry of Finance, which does not take the inherent fragility of those operators into account, does not allow any advance payment and stipulates all sorts of obligations that only public institutions with steady subsidy flow could fulfill.

In some countries the structural subsidy of larger and more important cultural institutions is allocated by authorities with an expectation that these institutions spend part of it on their international activities. How much they actually spend on such activities is rarely checked. Public cultural institutions in most countries still assume that international work is something *additional* to the domestic business as usual, and that the extra expenses it requires for travel, displacement, translation and related costs need to be compensated by the authorities with extra project subsidies. This is an argument that won't hold for too long, at least within the EU.

In contrast, smaller project organizations without any structural subsidy consider international engagement as essential part of their work, because it can bring them project subsidies from which they seek to cover some of their overhead expenses as well.

Besides national governments, with their ministries and specialized agencies, many public authorities on a regional and municipal level appear increasingly prepared to act as financiers of international cultural cooperation. Regions and cities have recognized international cultural cooperation for its developmental function and its benefit to audiences. In addition, they expect such forms of engagement to improve the image of the city or region and highlight its specificity and uniqueness. In some countries lower level public authorities are eager to challenge the prerogatives of the national government, or impose their own priorities, whether cultural or political. For smaller and less known cultural operators it is usually easier to approach local or regional public authorities and be recognized as qualified partners in international cultural cooperation meriting some financial support, than seeking to engage the national government's support.

In the post-communist countries of Central and Eastern Europe new autonomous operators with no structural support from their own government apply to foreign governments and their agencies for significant structural or development support under a temporary project label.

⌘   In the early 1990's, through the Theater Instituut Nederland the Dutch Ministry of Culture supported the development of contemporary dance in the Czech Republic—the Kylian Project, named after the well known Dutch choreographer of Czech origin, Jiřy Kylian. The Ministry supported the creation of Trafó, the first venue for contemporary dance in Budapest, in same manner. Via its MATRA program (acronym standing for "social transformation", aiming to bring citizens and public authorities closer to each other in post-communist countries), the Dutch Ministry of Foreign Affairs supported the development of Red House, an arts, culture and public debate center in Sofia, providing the core of its funding for several years.

Cultural operators approach a foreign embassy or foreign cultural institute in their city for financial support, but know that they have a chance only if their project contains a partnership link with someone in the cultural constellation of the same country.

⌘   In contrast, the Kulturstiftung des Bundes—the German federal cultural foundation, endowed by the government, has been distributing grants to foreign artists and cultural organizations in several countries, without the requirement of either a German angle, partner or a link with German cultural life. This is seen as an initial investment in the *capacity building* of the recipients for subsequent participation in international cultural projects. In another scheme, the same foundation funded a rich package of German–Hungarian and German–Polish cooperation projects of such considerable complexity and intensity that it was probably capable of creating some continuity in cross border engagement.

Intergovernmental organizations and programs

Those who work with their neighbors across national borders can in some cases hope to acquire some support from the intergovernmental funds for *regional cooperation*. The Nordic countries have institutionalized such a cooperation within the Nordic Council that has also spearheaded their cultural engagement with Poland and the newly independent Baltic countries throughout the 1990s. There is some critique from the practitioners on account of the Nordic Council's highly institutionalized modus operandi and its rather obsolete enclosure within the North European geographic space.

Cultural operators from Central Europe might seek to attract some funding from the Visegrád partnership between Hungary, the Czech Republic, Slovakia and Poland, set up at an early stage of their post-communist history, in the early 1990's, and to a great extent superseded by their present membership in the European Union, but still active in a limited way.

The Stability Pact for South Eastern Europe, signed with great pomp and circumstance by international leaders after the end of the wars in the former Yugoslavia, shamelessly omitted to name culture and international cultural cooperation alongside education, media and human rights, in its program. The omission is difficult to understand if one remembers to what extent ethnic hatred and animosity were generated in the years preceding the breakdown of Yugoslavia through cultural production, and how staunchly small groups of cultural operators consistently opposed war, xenophobia and nationalist propaganda. In practice, a few cultural projects have been supported by the Stability Pact provisions, but under some other creative heading and rationale.

Similarly, OSCE with its headquarters in Vienna has no specific cultural mandate but covers human rights and the media. This made it possible to assign small amounts to international projects of partly cultural nature in some rare instances.

⌘ At the end of 2005 the European Cultural Foundation and Dutch Hivos Foundation launched a Flexible Fund to support cultural capacity building and regional cooperation in the Western Balkan. They received some support from the Open Society Institute (OSI) and expect commitment of additional donors. The goal is to stimulate actions that will reinforce the cultural dimension of the region's slow and difficult integration in the EU.

Some intergovernmental initiatives are driven by a *common language*, spoken in several countries. Concerned with the worldwide dominance of the English language, the French government has committed significant resources to encourage projects reaffirming *francophonie*, linguistic ties amongst cultural professionals in different countries of Europe where French is one of the official languages (Belgium, Switzerland) or where it has strong traditional roots (Romania, Italy, Spain) and especially in the former French colonies in the developing world. There are frequently festivals of *francophonie* and in the large cultural center la Villette in Paris there is a theater venue dedicated to the foreign artistic expression of the French language.

⌘ In 2006, two associations, acting as extended arms of the French Ministry of Culture, AFAA (Association française de l'action artistique), charged since the 1930s with presenting French artists abroad, and ADPF (Association pour la diffusion de la pensée fran-çaise), since 1945 a promoter of French letters abroad, were sud-denly merged in a new organization, CulturesFrance (www. culturesfrance.com), expected to integrate French cultural engage-ment worldwide and raise the profile of French culture and language.

The Spanish government has developed similar initiatives based on the communality of the Spanish language, especially in Latin America. Portugal has supported collaborative cultural projects in the name of *lusitanidade*, the common sphere of Portuguese language encompassing Brazil, former colonies in Africa, Macao and Goa. The Nederlandse Taalunie, sustaining the unity of the Dutch language in the Netherlands and the Belgian region of Flanders, maintains support for translation, the training of foreign teachers of the Dutch language, but also aids common cultural initiatives of Dutch and Flemish cul-tural organizations (literature, drama) in third countries. The Taalunie has recently been officially joined by Surinam, a former Dutch colony.

During the Cold War, cultural cooperation under UNESCO's auspices was actively sought after by the so-called Soviet 'satellite' countries and after the collapse of Communism, UNESCO's operational activities in and for Central and Eastern Europe were stepped up, focusing on cultural heritage and cul-tural diversity. But the organization that today has 191 member states is inevi-tably a funder of only limited significance as regards cultural cooperation at the European level alone. However, it does promote trans-continental initia-tives which have an intercultural dimension and has in this way supported many efforts of this kind carried out by European actors.

After the end of the Cold War, practically all European countries became members of the Council of Europe, but its inclusiveness could not translate into growing political influence and operational capacity. While the Council initiated comparisons of national cultural policies, organized some trainings, published books on cultural policy, held debates and seminars and initially supported some of the emerging international cultural networks, in the late 1990s it lost much of its capacity to initiate further international cultural cooperation and fund specific projects. The thematic range of its cultural arm shrunk to just a few reflective and analytical initiatives such as intercultural dialogue, and even this topic was taken over by the European Commission, which declared 2008 the year of intercultural dialogue. Some historic achievements of the Council remain of lasting value, however, especially the articulation of internationally accepted standards and conventions in international cultural cooperation, pro-tection of cultural heritage and cultural rights of minorities.

European Union

The political prominence of the Council of Europe has been gradually overshadowed by the rise of the European Union. For many years, while the European Economic Community (the official name of the organization before it became the EU) was primarily an economic arrangement among member states, culture played no role in its work. Only after the end of the Cold War did culture acquire limited competence within the European Union, with the 1992 Maastricht Treaty and the inclusion of article 128 (later re-numerated as article 151) that stipulates a possibility of actions and programs in culture, in order to supplement what the national governments are doing—and only if they all agree. The competence domain is limited by the *subsidiarity* principle, requires *unanimity* of decisions, focuses on *non-commercial exchanges* and proclaims an ambition to create some *added European value* that remains a vague, never properly defined quality. Nevertheless, on the basis of this culture paragraph the EU has developed some limited regulation concerning the audiovisual sector, television, fixed book price and copyright. It has also launched programs such as Kaleidoscope and Ariadne in 1990's and Culture 2000 for the period 2000–2006. The development of a new culture specific program for the budgetary period 2007–2013 of the EU was delayed by the derailment of the European Constitution project in the referenda in France and the Netherlands in 2005, and a protracted dispute about the size and structure of the new 2007–2013 budget, resolved only in April 2006.

Despite miniscule budgetary means (in 2000–2006 only €34 million per year), vague objectives, cumbersome procedures and a heavy-handed managerial regime, Culture 2000 has in the recent years enabled many multilateral cooperation projects. In all, from 2000 to 2004 (further data are still unavailable!!!) the program made over one thousand grants, of which 90% were for year-long projects and some 10% for 3 year long partnerships. These grants always cover only part of the budget and are given on condition that the applicant partners can prove that they are fundraising for, or able to come up with the remaining funds needed. Despite the creation of a network of Cultural Contact Points, small service organizations attached to national ministries of culture and in some countries operating as autonomous agencies, charged with the task of helping operators prepare serious applications for the Culture 2000 program, this remains in practice an arduous, time consuming task. The majority of smaller operators have no capacity to fulfil all the complex applicants' preconditions and provide the guarantees required. The slowness of decision-making and delayed payments from Brussels make it practically impossible for many interested parties to use this program. Although the new EU culture program might bring about some modest improvements, the EU's administrative rules and practices remain at odds with the modus operandi, tempo and customary cash flow of many cultural operators in Europe and the total sum of €408 million, reserved for 2007–2013, corresponds in no way to the needs, interests and ambitions of operators in 27 countries of the EU and their colleagues in candidate states (Croatia, Macedonia, Turkey) and in countries of the European Economic Area (Island, Norway and Switzerland).

⌘ In the new cultural program, running from 2007, the European Union is aiding some organizations of 'European significance,' chiefly networks, and continues to support a small group of music ensembles that cleverly put "European" in their name (European Union Youth Orchestra, European Union Baroque Orchestra, European Youth Jazz Orchestra...) as 'European ambassadors.' In principle these ensembles could be seen as cooperative platforms since they are composed of musicians from different countries, but the EU support is chiefly driven by its own need for visibility.

In dealing with the European Union and its institutions many cultural operators have displayed formidable ingenuity and managed to obtain funds for international cultural cooperation from various EU schemes designated for *education* and *training* (Leonardo, Socrates, Gruntwig), *civil society* enhancement, *youth, employment, information* and *research*. The operators in the candidate countries were in rare instances able to receive some limited assistance for international cultural cooperation projects from EU funds aiming to facilitate transition, build capacities and prepare them for full membership. It will be especially important to watch how the EU will treat the Turkish candidacy (made official in 2004, with negotiations started in October 2005, and progressing haltingly) and how quickly Turkish cultural operators may be able to make use of some of the EU funds. For those operators whose countries are not even in the EU waiting room (South East and Eastern Europe), the Brussels funds have remained inaccessible, except in some rare instances, for specific educational programs.

⌘ The Budapest Observatory on financing of culture has been systematically monitoring the capacity of cultural operators in Central and Eastern Europe to access EU funding for cooperative projects, showing that the capacity build up to partake in these programs has been protracted and slow, that organizations from the region appear as partners, in multilateral projects but rarely as the *leading* partner.

European Comission has declared 2008 a year of *intercultural dialogue* and set aside some 10 million euro for high visibility events and media campaign, expecting more through the engagement of member states, regions, cities and private sources.

Much of the EU budget lies in the so-called *structural funds*, which aim to reduce the disparity of socio-economic conditions in which EU citizens live, as measured per region rather than by country. Before 2004, Greece, Spain, Portugal and Ireland profited greatly from these funds used for their infrastructural development, urban revitalization and some rural investment. The expectation is that much of the flow of those funds will shift towards the new member states in Central Europe, but that the funds available will yield fewer euros per inhabitant, require more national resources and be run on a stricter regime of criteria. So far some of the structural funds have been occasionally applied to the development of cultural infrastructure, with a rationale that this will boost the chances of cultural tourism and some training support. Since those funds seek to improve conditions in a given region, they cannot have a direct benefit for international cultural cooperation. But they could help develop or revitalize facilities (cultural centers, residencies, venues, museums, etc.) that may in turn one day be engaged in international cultural projects.

Application for those funds and their management relies on local authorities and not on Brussels officials. There is a very long bottom up process, lasting several years, to articulate priorities and predefine the fields and the kind of applicable projects. If, for instance, the renovation of former industrial buildings for cultural purposes is not included among the priorities of a multiannual general plan, it cannot benefit from those funds later on. Cultural operators need to secure in time their own places for pariticipation in a consultative process where local and regional authorities seek to define priorities and program fields in dialogue with the business community, civil society, unions and other interested parties. If they neglect to insert their input early on, they will not be able to benefit from the structural funds attributed to their territory.

The European Union has increasingly been concerned about its relationship with some of its geographical neighbors, especially in the Mediterranean area, from where there is a strong migratory pressure, much economic activity restricted by EU protectionist policies (especially in agricultural export) and a long common political and cultural history from antiquity to decolonization. The *Barcelona process* was initiated in 1995 as a flow of initiatives, fora, networks and projects, all aiming to enhance EU-Mediterranean cooperation in various fields and especially in respect of democracy and human rights, civil society, education and culture. The EU even reserved a considerable amount of euros for regional cooperation, to be spent through its MEDA program over a number of years, but the outbreak of the Palestinian *first intifada* caused most of the Barcelona process budget to be frozen. Subsequently, the *second intifada* and anti-terrorism measures initiated by the EU after 9/11 shifted the preferred instruments from development investment towards an investment in security. From 1995 to 2003, MEDA committed €5,458 billion in co-operation programs while the European Investment Bank lent €14 billion for developing activities of the Euro-Mediterranean partners since 1974 (€3.7 billion in 2002-2003). MEDA II covered the period 2000-2006 and amounted €5.35 billion. Yet, only a miniscule part of those funds went to culture, and efforts made to revive the Barcelona process in 2005 stalled on the resistance of some Arab governments to the empowerment of NGOs in their countries.

International cultural cooperation from the EU with partners in the southern Mediterranean countries remains difficult and has become even worse since their already poor mobility has been further affected by the additional harshness of the EU visa regime. The Anna Lindh Euro-Mediterranean Foundation for Dialogue Between Cultures (endowed with a start-up grant of the European Commission of €5 million under the MEDA program) was created by the 25 Member States of the European Union and their ten Mediterranean partners (from Turkey to Morocco, but including also Israel) and became operational in 2005, set up in the new Alexandrine Library in Alexandria, Egypt. Its budget is very modest, and the decision-making procedure is encumbered by the numerous member states implicated and the political sensitivities of some of their governments. The Foundation still has to prove its usefulness for the enhancement of international cultural cooperation in this crucial but volatile region, marked by a great disparity of cultural infrastructure and the freedom of cultural operators to organise themselves. Its first call for proposals (2006) contained a range of conventionally defined priorities, driven by specific artistic disciplines rather than some transversal issues. Some events that were to be hosted by the Foundation have been cancelled abruptly.

The model for the Anna Lindh foundation has in fact been borrowed from the Asia-Europe Foundation, set up in 1997, in Singapore, by members of the EU and ASEAN (Association of Southeast Asian Nations). This foundation has funded a few projects and network development in cultural heritage, contributed to a few meetings of European and Asian artists and is preparing to launch an internet portal on European-Asian cultural cooperation opportunities. Again, its funds are very modest and its decision making board is slow and complex because of the intergovernmental structure bringing together representatives from almost 40 countries. Yet, in June 2007, the European Commissioner for Education and Culture announced his intention to set up a platform for cooperation with Africa, Pacific and Carribean.

Despite its complex range of programs and labyrinthine rules and requirements, the European Union remains a major source of funding for various forms of multilateral cultural cooperation and it will in all probability continue to play this role, now that the dispute about the 2007–2013 budget has been resolved. At a time when the EU lacks a clear sense of direction and cannot pool out a reserve scenario to replace the failed European Constitution project, when politicians hesitate how much of a political community they should try to shape on top of a functioning common market, culture might appear to some as a marginal issue. To others, however, it appears as a realm where new self-confidence and sense of communality could be built and affirmed. For cultural operators in Europe, the EU remains a difficult, oblique, not at all user-friendly but nevertheless strategically important funding source. In the view of European cultural operators and their advocacy organizations such as EFAH, even if the volume of resources available for international cultural cooperation cannot be spectacularly raised before 2014, the focus and the quality of the EU programs and the transparency and efficiency of their administration could and should be improved.

9

PRIVATE FUNDING AND ALTERNATIVE FINANCING

Despite the preponderance of various public sources of funding, described in the previous chapter, private support for international cultural cooperation deserves special attention as a field of much potential growth. Several major modes of funding will be examined here, with the notions of *private-public partnership* and *cultural entrepreneurship* probed at the very end of the chapter.

Foundations

There are hundreds of private foundations across Europe, set up by rich individuals, families and private business corporations and in some exceptional cases by governments themselves: Fondation de France by the French government, Prince Claus Fonds by the Dutch government, King Baudouin by the Belgian government. Many of them give grants for scientific, educational and social causes, and a minority also for cultural projects. A commitment to the development of young talent and shaping of international partnerships is more an exception than a rule among these foundations.

⌘ In a recent study conducted by the Fondazione Fitzcarraldo of Turin, *Cultural Cooperation in Europe: What Role for Foundations?*, it has become clear that only a tiny minority among several hundreds of private foundations in Europe sees international cultural cooperation as one of their fields of engagement. Some foundations are contemplating those issues but feel that they lack proper insights and competent staff in order to set their priorities and develop funding schemes. Others prefer to leave this field to public authorities, fearing political entanglements and controversy. Many do award prizes for exemplary cultural achievements, but even if they occasionally have a foreign laureate, that could hardly be called international cultural cooperation.

⌘ The European Cultural Foundation, already mentioned in the first chapter, exemplifies a remarkable exception in its understanding of Europe as an integrated cultural space. It has developed and spun off various initiatives, programs and institutions in its long history and after the end of the Cold War developed new programs in Central and Eastern Europe and sought openings and effective approaches to the difficult cultural constellations in the Southern Mediterranean. As with many other foundations, ECF too shifted from a reactive mode of cooperation—waiting for interesting applications and allocating grants to the best ones—to its own programming priorities, development of partnerships through grant giving and stimulation of multilateral projects (Arts for Social Change and Kultura Nova programs), training of public officials for cultural policy (Policies for Culture) and emphasis on individual mobility throughout Europe with its Apex and Step Beyond programs. In recent years the Foundation added cultural policy advocacy on a European level to its core activities.

For many smaller cultural operators it is difficult to reach major foundations that prefer to deal with large institutional grant seekers and elaborate long-term funding relationships with them. Some foundations set up by rich individuals and families remain deliberately outside public attention, operating in relative obscurity, with unclear priorities and focus. It is hard for a novice cultural operator to discern, which of those foundations might perhaps be interested in considering an application. Some smaller foundations are not only reclusive but also slow and poorly responsive in their communication. Their position is differently regulated across Europe, the tax benefits also vary and not all national legislations oblige them to ensure transparency and some minimum public communication about their assets and spending.

⌘ In southern Europe, beside some tycoon family foundations (Alexander S. Onassis Public Benefit Foundation and Lambrakis Foundation in Greece, Agnelli Fondation in Italy, Leventis Foundation in Cyprus), there are some traditional banking foundations, sometimes set up by the banks under a legal obligation derived from an assumption that banks make extra profits. They operate chiefly in

Spain (La Caixa) and Italy where 88 banking foundations were established around year 2000, but very few of them include support to international cooperation, also because they have legal constraints in funding activities abroad. The only actor on the international scene is La Compagnia di San Paolo. In Northern Europe, there is also the The Bank of Sweden Tercentenary Foundation in Stockholm, a major research fund, which has recently moved into international cultural cooperation. And several banking families in Turkey have set up their foundations with a strong cultural mandate (Vebhi Koç Foundation, Yapi Kredi Cultural Activities, Arts and Publishing, Vaksa – The Sabanci Foundation), as well as their own galleries, museums and cultural centers. On Cyprus, the Bank of Cyprus Foundation and the Laiki Group should be named in this context.

⌘   In Portugal, during the dictatorship, that is until 1974, there was practically no public cultural policy and the Calouste Gulbenkian Foundation with its enormous wealth offered considerable compensation for the non-existent public services, funding research, education, mobile libraries, contemporary arts as some sort of virtual monopoly. Today, with more public engagement and other private players, Gulbenkian is still a major source of cultural funding but no longer a lonely giant.

⌘   George Soros' Open Society Institute, mentioned in the first chapter, practically withdrew from Central and Eastern Europe even before the EU Enlargement and from Russia as well. It has maintained for a while a limited engagement, also in culture, in South East Europe (Serbia, Montenegro, Kosovo, Bosnia and Herzegovina, Macedonia) and revived its attention for emancipation and cultural integration of Roma in Europe. Soros is much interested in the development of civil society in Caucasus, Turkey, post-Soviet Central Asia and China and OSI Arts and Culture Network Program supports projects in Central Asian countries. In 2006 George Soros established the OSI Europe foundation in order to affirm the values of an open society within the EU and counter Euroscepticism and outright anti-European sentiments in some new member states.

⌘   In Germany, foundations allied to political parties (Adenauer-Stiftung/ demo-christians, Ebert-Striftung/ socialdemocrats...), financed by public money on the basis of the election results of their respective parties, engage in a great range of programs that focus on political education, but occasionally touch on culture, in Germany and abroad.

⌘   Business corporations have set up major foundations in Germany (Volkswagen, Bosch, Bertelsmann, etc.) or run their own arts program (Siemens). Such foundations appear since recently in Southern Europe as well, either operating at arm's length from the parent company and pursuing their own agenda in an autonomous way, with own assets and resources, or functioning as real ice-breakers, supporting the operations of the parent company in opening up new markets.

⌘   Some of the UK charities derive from 19th century origins, and across Europe one encounters charitable foundations linked to the Catholic and Protestant churches, but with a limited interest in culture, understood chiefly as cultural heritage preservation, religiously inspired visual arts and religious music.

⌘   Foundations have also been set up by members of European aristocratic and ruling families or on their behalf, and some are endowed by a steady contribution of lottery income: the Prins Bernhard Cultuurfonds has been operating for 60 years on Dutch lottery income, but has doubled its spending through the endowment contributions made to it by private individuals for some specific purposes of the donor's choice.

⌘   Accelerating capital formation in Central Europe in the transition from a communist to market economy has not so far brought many grant giving foundations. The opportunities for further re-investment and expansion have obviously been more of a priority than the assignment of capital for foundation endowment. Murky and constantly changing tax regulations have created another obstacle for the emergence of new foundations. The Kulczyk foundation in Poland runs its own cultural center in a Poznan shopping mall, and the Batory Foundation in Warsaw, a recipient of George Soros' largesse in the past, continues with its endowment building and grant distribution after Soros' departure from Poland and emphasizes spending outside major cities. In Russia, some newly made tycoons have created their own foundations for a variety of purposes, including nominally culture, but the serial emigration of tycoons from Russia under the Putin presidency and especially the dramatic turnaround of Khodorkovsky and his business and philanthropic empire indicate the extreme volatility of Russian capitalism, as well as the legal limitations and political pressures brought on the NGOs.

These examples should be seen only as an indication of a broad range of programming priorities, financial arrangements and political circumstances that exist among foundations in Europe. Foundations often display conservative attitudes, are slow to respond to the changing constellations or tend to favor cultural heritage over contemporary creativity, especially in an international context. On the other hand, for a private foundation with a strong leadership and self-confident board, in principle it could be easier to re-arrange programming priorities and assert itself in new fields and themes, without the complicated political pressures and prolonged debates that burden the priority reallocation of public funds. Various foundations' networks, informal clubs and the European Foundation Centre (EFC) in Brussels would be the best points of entry for the European organizations in culture that advocate more foundation spending on international cultural cooperation.

Sponsorship

Sponsorship is often paraded as a panacea for reduced public spending in culture. After more than 20 years of business sponsorship in arts and culture, it has not become a substantial alternative to public funding anywhere in Europe. Moreover, pan-European sponsorship in particular did not take off, mainly because of the differences between national markets, consumers' attitudes and divergent tax advantages. Calculations of how much business sponsorship is really involved in culture alongside public spending and private foundation grants are complicated by divergent notions of culture. Careful analysis would in all probability show a clear bifurcation between sponsorship of mass entertainment events (rock concerts, for instance) and sponsorship of high culture/high prestige programs, such as block buster exhibitions in top museums and classical music concerts with star conductors, singers and instrumentalists in very fancy music halls. Most cultural operators seeking funds for international cooperation would fit neither of these two categories. Lesser known, experimental, controversial and critical projects, reaching only a limited audience, cannot appeal too much to prospective sponsors who seek safe (i.e. traditional/conventional), popular, prestigious and mainstream events as vehicles to give them exposure and visibility. Specific circumstances, political contingencies and long term thinking sometimes prompt international corporations to sponsor rather unusual projects, such as foreign theater productions about HIV/AIDS prevention in South Africa, where some of the sponsors feel a moral responsibility to compensate for their long association with the apartheid regime.

⌘ Sponsorship is opportunity driven. China is a hot topic, politically and economically, an emerging superpower that provokes fascination and anxiety but whose traditional and especially contemporary cultures are not much known in Europe. Hence the Amsterdam China festival, held in October 2005, initiated by the Concertgebouw and joined by some 30 other cultural organizations, all of them offering something from China or Chinese, from concerts to exhibits and films, through performances to lectures, videos and symposia, has had little trouble in acquiring sponsorship from major Dutch and international corporations active in China: Philips, the Schiphol Group, TNT, Price-WaterhouseCoopers, Fortis bank and Akzo Nobel chemical concern, aided by the media sponsorship of the daily newspaper *de Volkskrant* and the NPS television network. All of these were willing to be associated with this mega-event, while the chain of department stores De Bijenkorf arranged a special floor with consumers' items from China.

Many international performing arts festivals are doing quite well with sponsors. If they can sell 30–70 thousand tickets in 2–4 weeks and offer a mix of smaller and bigger, more exclusive and more accessible performances from various countries popping up at various locations in the same city, they can usually attract sponsors with an orientation towards the affluent, easy spending, outgoing younger public. Communication and media, travel and especially mobile phone and software companies find festivals quite attractive. Banks sponsor in order to attract new, younger clients and small businesses offer sponsorship in kind.

⌘ Again, specific economic conditions in Russia, or rather in Moscow, have prompted the Sbir bank and Nestlé to compete ferociously for main sponsorship of the Golden Mask Performing Arts Festival that features the best Russian drama, dance and opera productions and in addition attracts many foreign professionals with its Russian show case of emerging artistic groups. The bank won, yet Nestlé did not withdraw but continued to offer the public in the theater lobbies instant coffee during intermission, seeking to establish a new habit.

⌘   The LIFT Festival in London broke new ground when it developed its LIFT Business Forum in association with the *Financial Times* in the 1990s. It offered highly placed corporate executives tickets to festival performances along with all the usual champagne, but added a series of exclusive seminars with the top artists, who then spoke about the usual items of routine management seminars from their unique artistic perspective: leadership, stress management, risk taking, intercultural competence, job satisfaction and motivation. LIFT's income from a 4000 pound fee (almost €6000) per participant was modest because of the limited number of participants such seminars can accommodate, but most of them became loyal LIFT admirers and advocates later, and kept recruiting new sponsors in their business network, thus creating a long-term benefit for the festival.

Festivals and other cultural operators complain about the instability of sponsorship relationships, their tendency to go away after a year for a variety of reasons connected with change of personnel on the top, a downturn in the business climate, reorganization, takeover or just a new appealing sponsorship opportunity arising elsewhere. A new, long and time consuming search for a replacement sponsor ensues. The appeal that the festivals provoke among sponsors has also led to a rapid increase in the number of festivals, often one-off rather than recurring events, programs packaged in a festival formula and given an attractive name, primarily for marketing and fundraising reasons. For most of the smaller project-driven cultural operators working on an international scale sponsorship is an exceptional opportunity rather then a regular source of funding. The presenters, accommodating programs from abroad within a carefully balanced season, are better conditioned to recruit sponsors because of their familiarity with the local market and prolonged exposure in it, while the artists traveling with their work abroad appeal much less to potential sponsors.

Public-private partnership

In the USA, most cultural organizations enjoy no public support and survive on the foundation grants and donations of wealthy individuals and loyal patrons. In times of crisis individuals who sit on the boards of cultural organizations are expected to write a generous check in order to ease cash flow. The system of individual patronage and donation is less established in Europe, even in the countries that offer some (even if less generous) fiscal benefits for such largesse. To borrow money from a bank or from relatives in order to realize some international project is also not common and the banks would be reluctant to aid such risky ventures. Reliance on some form of public funding still remains the major option, despite shrinking or stagnating public budgets, with the search for foundation funding and sponsorship coming next. The much touted *public-private partnership* is a rather vague concept. In most cases it is an euphemism for the withdrawal of public responsibility for cultural production and distribution in the hope that private capital will come in to foot the bill. More ideologically, the concept implies that public policy creates some general conditions and dynamics for cultural production, but the operational risk is passed on to private capital. Usually, where there is a willingness to take a risk there must be an expectation of possible profit as well and therefore the private-public partnership concept engineers a shift from a non-profit to a for-profit culture.

⌘   Not always, however. The European Cultural Foundation has been pursuing the idea of an *observatory* for international cultural co-operation, first mentioned in the MEP Giorgio Ruffolo's report to the European Parliament and in a subsequent parliamentary resolution (2001) that sought 'to consider culture as an essential element in European integration, particularly in the context of the expansion of the Union'. Finally in 2005 the Lab for Culture was launched as a 4 year long pilot project, co-financed by the European Commission, several national governments of EU member states and a few major foundations. The Lab is expected to facilitate the access of new operators to funds, know-how, partners and good practices, run a complex web portal with information and analysis, and conduct several research programs, all with a goal to make international cultural cooperation more dynamic and inclusive, more effective and better funded.

Public-private partnership occurs more frequently in some infrastructural development than in the operational project management. After minister of culture Veltroni, in the center-left Italian government, signed the first agreement with Confindustria, the private business lobby, he pushed a complicated and controversial bill through on the 'privatisation' of the opera houses in 1996, which turns them into foundations, dependent on both public and private support. Some years later, the Berlusconi 2 government in Italy has sought private parties, i.e. commercial companies, to lease heritage buildings and manage state museums, without setting any minimum standards in conducting the core museum tasks and providing quality public service. In international cultural cooperation, public bodies sometimes *sub-contract* private companies (for-profit or non-profit) to carry out some representational tasks or organize some events of a promotional character abroad, where subcontracting replaces a grant-giving letter. The difference could be more formal than substantial.

⌘ A 38, a former Ukrainian stone schleper, converted into a fancy events boat anchored in Budapest, on the Danube shore, has been launched by a for-profit company that took out a loan from a bank to pay for an expensive and prolonged rebuilding. The boat is a popular destination for concerts, debates, corporate events, press conferences and receptions. A non-profit organization, linked to the founding company, seeks subsidies for specific cultural events and occasionally tenders its services to be contracted by public authorities. The experience shows that tendering, selection, contracting and payment go faster and more smoothly than in a subsidy relationship.

Cultural entrepreneurship

Budgets made for international cooperative projects practically always count on some earned income. The problem is that in most cases this income does not cover total expenses. Operators seek to reduce expenses without hurting the quality of the product and to increase earned income with some auxilliary activities or products, such as merchandizing items or sale of subsidiary rights. The former is risky, and demands some operating capital, while the latter works only if there are some takers. Cultural organizations with their own public space (venues, concert halls, cultural centers, etc.) do seek additional sources of income, running a café or a bar or renting space for commercial events and corporate functions. The income generated in this way could enable international cooperation projects as partners' own investment. The project itself, with its complex logistic and relatively short exploitation/shelf life, usually cannot earn much and allows for little in the way of supplementary activities that would be income generating.

The motivation of participants in international projects is often much stronger than their rational calculation of labor invested vs. remuneration received. They still take part in a project for a very small fee or none at all, but seek to balance their own personal budget by working later or in parallel in some more lucrative job or project. In some fields and professions there is an expectation that sacrifices made at the beginning of a career could ultimately be richly rewarded: a music group dreams of commercial contracts, a designer of a lucrative contract with a manufacturer, an actor or composer of a film contract that pays much better. Similarly, non-profit cultural organizations seek some money-making activities or services in order to generate the capital needed to subsidize international cooperation. Whatever is earned is always reinvested in future projects and the current deficits are offset against expected income in coming years. International cultural cooperation rests on some determined, modest, self-sacrificing and at the same time quite bussiness-like individuals who take considerable artistic and financial risks, extrapolate their balance sheet well into the future and systematically underpay and overwork themselves and their companions for the sake of the collaborative product and presumed cultural and social capital it is expected to create.

Those who run international cultural projects consciously stretch the resources of their non-profit organization, taking a calculated risk: even a financially loss-making project could bring much satisfaction and inspiration, endowing the organization and those individuals involved with prestige and distinction, offering professional growth and new insights, skills and know-how. These relatively abstract and vague gains need to be balanced against more concrete and prosaic losses and in turn compensated for in the next project or simply written off. A cultural entrepreneur of international orientation is a professional who has a clear, unsentimental overview of these contradictions, and succeeds in carrying them from one project into another, preserving the gains and reducing the losses. When the entrepreneur gets exhausted in this struggle, or even crushed and leaves the game, a new generation of operators usually stands ready to take over and assert its own method of continuous risk taking. Looking back at the past 18 years since the end of the Cold War, one sees an explosive growth of ambition and willingness to engage in international cultural cooperation and the realization of a growing volume of increasingly complex projects despite shrinking public expenditure, rising costs, growing commercial pressures and a preponderance of internationally distributed industrial entertainment.

120

10

TRENDS IN INTERNATIONAL CULTURAL COOPERATION

An overview of the various forms of international cultural cooperation presented in chapter 4 indicated that these forms are becoming increasingly ambitious and complex. For most producers and presenters involvement in something international even in the not so distant past used to be a rather exceptional opportunity, but today many work internationally as a matter of daily routine. They have more experience and self-confidence and an expanded personal network, so the ambition to invent original, protracted and complicated models grows as well.

From incidental
to continuous

If partners have a good experience with each other in a specific international project, they will at some point seek opportunities to work together again. This might alter the nature of their relationship, as *protracted* partnership in several projects tends to build up a privileged position and rely on accumulated trust and shared experience. In some cases, they could become regular partners. Think of a presenter-producer who regularly handles each new premiere of an artistic group or provides a steady station on the European tours of a non-European company.

⌘   DeSingel in Antwerp is an obligatory stop on each European tour of the Canadian dance company Lalala Human Steps.

⌘   The Estonian Dance Agency works with a few regular partners in arranging tours of Estonian contemporary dance companies in the Baltic region.

⌘   Sophiensæle in Berlin works regularly with the Grand Theater Groningen on developing some dance pieces of new choreographers who do not have to be Dutch or German at all. What matters is that the leaders of both venues believe in their talent and potential.

⌘   Several festivals, such as Festival d'Avignon, KunstenFESTI-VALdesArts in Brussels and Aarhus Festuge feel a strong commitment to some artists and seek to present each of their new works.

⌘   Theater an der Ruhr in Mülheim an der Ruhr has a long history of relations with the Municipal Theater in Istanbul that evolved from mutual guest performances into repeated co-productions.

If collaboration becomes significant and essential for the functioning of partners, it evolves into an international *strategic* partnership. The complementary relationship and synergy of the partners makes them more effective in carrying out their mission.

⌘   Theater Instituut Nederland in Amsterdam and the Vlaams Theater Instituut in Brussels worked very closely between 1992 and 2000 in presenting their performing artists and especially dramatic literature in the common Dutch language in third countries. They collaborated in research, publications, professional conferences for the Dutch and Flemish performing arts professionals and on several European projects, such as the conferences on the dissemination of plays written in smaller languages (Antwerp 1993, Ljubljana 1997).

⌘   The European Forum for the Arts and Heritage, an advocacy organization based in Brussels, and European Cultural Foundation, based in Amsterdam, conduct joint campaigns and actions to develop and profile Europe-wide cultural policy, especially geared to the EU institutions and member states' governments. ECF is able to take along several prominent private foundations while EFAH mobilizes international networks, national advocacy organizations and professional associations.

From presenting to (co-)producing

The loyalty of a presenter to a foreign artist or a group leads to a reoccurring presentation and then the role perhaps deepens and the presenter becomes a producer or a co-producer. In practice, that could mean that a venue hosts a foreign artist or a group for a protracted length of time and facilitates the making of a new production, stages its premiere, even organizes the subsequent international touring, instead of just booking the production made elsewhere for one or two nights. This shift is most visible in the practice of numerous festivals in Europe that are no longer satisfied with just the role of presenter of carefully chosen productions made elsewhere, but insist on producing and premiering new works. The impulse is to create something out of a series, to engineer a collaborative relationship that normally would not occur, to bring together artists who, because of their background, radius and domestic circumstances would perhaps never find each other and be able to work together.

⌘ Festival d'Avignon has changed its formula and for the last few years it has appointed for each edition a key artist as the main guest. This was Thomas Ostermeier in 2004, Jan Fabre in 2005, Josef Nadj in 2006 and Frédéric Fisbach in 2007. These artists are involved in the selection of other productions on the program, according to their esthetic predilections and affinities, and the festival co-produces new work in conjuction with them and from their circle of favorite artists.

From bilateral to multilateral

For a long time the dominant scope of international cultural cooperation has been marked by *bilateralism*, a relationship between two mutually committed partners. The root is in the primary exchange model and the tendency of public authorities to conduct their foreign policy in a set of bilateral engagements, often deploying cultural instruments to help achieve their goals. For less experienced cultural operators having just one foreign partner in a cooperative project might be complicated enough. One sees, however, a fast rise of multilateral international cultural projects, usually bringing together three to seven partners from various countries. The shift has probably been partially prompted by the requirements of the EU's cultural programs. In order to do something that goes beyond the engagement of national governments, firmly anchored in a bilateral logic, EU programs require that the grant application come from several partners from different countries. Otherwise EU involvement would have been difficult to justify in terms of its limited legal competence. The assumption made here is that 5 partners united around a common project automatically deliver the famous *added European value*. In practice, this is not necessarily so since some projects bring together several partners from various countries, but are realized in one single place and achieve only a very local impact.

Multilateral projects spring also from the practice of international cultural networks that bring together a great number of practitioners, nurture collegiality, professional appreciation and recognition of common goals, values and approaches in everyday work. On the basis of professional closeness and affinity nurtured within network practices, several potential partners gradually converge and gravitate towards each other and with the mutual trust that ties them together they start inventing some common projects, or consider joining an initiative of one of them. Multilateral cooperation is more complicated than bilateral, and involves more risks. Finding a common objective and defining a core for the project is more difficult and time consuming with more than just two partners; with more chances that disagreements could arise, that partners will disappoint each other, that someone will not carry out their own tasks as expected. Narcissism, arrogance and insensitivity towards others loom as dangers. The partner taking the role of the chief executive has more obligations and must supervise several components, tasks and partners, watch the multiple directions of expenditure and protect the agreed budget from diverse assaults. Internal divisions could also occur.

Despite all these rather obvious risks and inevitable complications, multilateral projects attract operators for their capacity to realize more ambitious, complex and costly projects; pool resources of the collaborating partners, engage in broader fundraising with multiple but separate national sources, and also split the inherent risks among the partners—an important assurance in a rather volatile creative process where the danger of artistic failure is always a threat. But beside artistic failure there are other external factors that can adversely affect a project: budgetary overspending, subsidies promised but never paid out or substantially delayed, permits canceled or refused; strikes; bad weather provoking cancellation of open air performances or reducing the expected audience size and dozens of other possible disasters. With several partners grouped around the project the chances of survival are better, setbacks can be compensated for and imbalances corrected. A multilateral setup promises more exposure, longer exploitation period and amplified impact.

Some operators claim that the learning benefit is higher in a multilateral project than in a bilateral one because participants are confronted with more compressed and concentrated cultural, professional and systemic differences to grasp and deal with, thus their intercultural competence is intensively challenged and perfected, the understanding of distinct professional traditions, routines and procedures grows and the differences among various national cultural systems manifest themselves sharply along the way. For all the participants such a project offers opportunities to reflect on the specificity of their own objectives and approach, own position in the domestic context, in contrast to those of all others involved. Partners learn in an intensive manner how to distinguish a simple misunderstanding from a principled disagreement and how to overcome both. Beyond the achievements of the project itself, multilateral partnership works as a major boost to the professional development of all parties involved.

From networks to consortia

Despite the success of international cultural networks that function as an essential infrastructure for international cooperation, there are sometimes visible signs of *networking fatigue*. Especially seasoned networkers, who have achieved their initial goals for which they joined a network, at some point, consider distancing themselves from the hustle and bustle of the gatherings that have, because of their appeal and successfulness, grown rather big. This size itself is a big pull factor for newcomers who expect to be successful in fishing for ideas, partners, funding and other opportunities in a rather big fish pond. For the more accomplished operators size could become an irritant: they know their place, and know quite well who the other relevant players within the network are, whom they like and respect and whom not, with whom they have a shared history of positive and not so positive experiences and whom they would trust in a new project.

⌘ The study *How Networking Works*, conducted by the Fondazione Fitzcarraldo of Turin (2001), commissioned by the network IETM, carefully analyzed the internal dynamic of a network and the flow of members in and out in relation to their primary motivations and advanced agendas. The Italian researchers identified some

125

crucial phases and patterns of interaction of the network's members, from joining to exit, and concluded that there is much enthusiasm and instinctive solidarity with professional peers in the behavior of operators, but also a dosage of pragmatism in assessing the optimal proportion of effort and cost invested in the network and expected benefits.

It has been mentioned in chapter 6 that international networks have the capacity to spin off other, more specialized networks. To this it should be added that in recent years some larger and more successful networks have demonstrated a capacity to spin off also some *consortia*, groups of members who repeatedly engage in multilateral cooperation. These are usually more seasoned and stronger operators who seek partners appropriate to themselves and their high standards and ambitions. These could be the starting premises for a consortium's formation, but in practice consortia also evolve and usually accommodate a rather diverse range of partners in terms of size, economic power experience and outreach, as the example of Theorem shows.

⌘   Theorem has emerged as a consortium from the network IETM on the initiative of the Avignon Festival director Bernard Faivre d'Arcier in 1998. His idea was to create a construction bringing together a few European presenters, mainly venues and festivals, who would be able to organize a thorough search for new emerging talent in Central and Eastern Europe, identify promising directors and enable them to make good productions, that is—help create decent production conditions with additional funding, and then let them tour in Western Europe, among the consortium members. This is another instance of presenters switching to the role of co-producers in order to satisfy their own demands and ambitions. Theorem combined the considerable resources of its members and acquired additional national and EU funds from the Culture 2000 program, so that it could undertake a thorough search for emerging talent, whether in the established repertory companies or in newly emerging autonomous production units. However, the concept was one-sided: it never envisaged facilitating tours through Central and Eastern Europe, but only from there westward. Soon Theorem members discovered that there is directorial talent in the region they prospected, but also a lack of strong production and touring management competence, so consequently management and stage technique seminars were organized. As the original consortium grew to over 20 members, with partners from all sides of Europe joining, the principle was modified: if four member organizations of the consortium were interested in the project, their own investment would be supplemented with the pool of resources raised by the consortium as a whole. In time, with the changes of personnel in some of the founding members, the interests and focus were modified. Coordination moved from Paris to Riga to be hosted by the New Theater Institute of Latvia. Smaller organizations from Central and Eastern Europe who joined the consortium later discovered that they could apply the working method to facilitate touring in their own part of Europe and at the same time continue working together, even if some of the founding members withdrew to pursue other interests. Theorem officially terminated its activity in 2006, but cooperation among some of its members continues.

The members of Theorem considered themselves mainly as a network but have in fact expanded the usual network practice of information exchange, reflection and debate to a consortium type of operation: they shared goals and responsibilities, pooled resources and repeatedly engaged in multilateral partnership among themselves. A similar shift from networking practice to consortium formation and engagement in a series of multilateral projects can be seen in other networks in a variety of fields including, besides arts, cultural heritage (museums), professional arts education (within the ELIA, European League of Institutes of the Arts) and cultural policy research.

⌘ In CIRCLE (Cultural Information and Research Centres Liaison in Europe), a network of cultural policy researchers, the annual meetings looking at one chosen topic have been based on its mapping within the members' own national cultural systems. More recently some CIRCLE members have been working more closely together, around a series of research projects in cultural policy. ERICARTS (European Institute for Comparative Cultural Research) in Bonn is such a consortium, derived from CIRCLE and there are some others in a more informal state of formation.

⌘ A good example of a network as a complex structured environment is the European Textile Network, a material-based international network whose membership comprises the whole range of stakeholders concerned with textile production: individuals, community groups, interest groups, business, public sectors, independent arts organizations, educational institutes. The eventual formation of the consortium reflects this complexity and focuses on some more specific interests.

⌘ The EUnetArt network for artistic work for and with children and adults has been stimulating collaborative ties among its members, but when a few started working together on a more stable basis, in a series of multilateral projects, this development destabilized the small network, creating a division between members plugged into the consortium and those feeling left out.

Consortium formation is a normal process in the evolution of international cooperation and it does not negatively affect larger networks where even several intertwined consortia might operate simultaneously without reducing the networking benefit for all the others. In smaller networks, however, emerging consortia might have a destabilizing and even divisive impact on others, whereas if the consortium's formation is delayed or fails for whatever reason, this might weaken the network itself—as in the Comedia network, where it happened that the focus on the intercultural dimension of performing arts never reached the consortium phase.

⌘ Soros Centers for Contemporary Art were formed in a rather hasty and intensive manner in the early 1990s as an offshoot of the Open Society Institute within the George Soros' system of philanthropic institutions. These were an addition to the national foundations in Central and Eastern European countries and one of the regional initiatives such as those launched by the OSI for media, publishing, arts and culture, Roma, etc. The Centers were expected to document contemporary visual arts production, organize exhibitions and additional activities and help reduce the international isolation of their visual artists. The Centers saw themselves as a network and yet sought to operate as a consortium too hastily, even before first taking time to consolidate themselves at home and as a network. They were quite numerous but not of the same strength or competence, some in strained relations with their own national Soros foundation, and lacking sufficient mutual trust and articulated affinity to be able to operate as a consortium. When Soros decided to terminate their core funding, the network itself became unsustainable. A few centers managed to survive with alternative financing and sought to reach the consortium formation phase only later, after some institutional stabilization and more networking practice.

In several European cities such as Paris, Brussels and Amsterdam, foreign government's cultural centers have sought to organize themselves as a consortium and undertake joint projects in the country they cover. In Amsterdam they even formed a legal non-profit entity and sought the regular 4 years funding from the Dutch Ministry of Culture (OCW) as many Dutch cultural organizations do. They did not receive it. Some of them sought to apply to the European Commission's Culture 2000 program as if they were autonomous operators from different countries and not parts of several governmental cultural promotion agencies. In some instances they succeeded in organizing some events together, a program of orchestrated and packaged performances, film and video projections, concerts, exhibitions, debates and workshops, in collaboration with the local partners, but they have not succeeded in becoming a functioning consortium with prolonged impact and engagement because they lack full operational autonomy, depend on their own governments' instructions, priorities and bureaucratic procedures that are often mutually incompatible. Due to their original promotional orientation they tend to compete among themselves about the visibility of their input rather than collaborate.

⌘　There are 40 foreign cultural centers and institutes in Paris. They present national governments, some regions (Catalonia, Wallonia, Anatolia), broad geographic and cultural zones (the Arab world, Latin America) and diasporic communities (Kurds, Armenians). Together they created a "forum" aiming to enhance their collaboration and open a multilateral space for reflection. In practice, every center has its own programming, and even though there is a common program brochure, highlighting a week of many events in the autumn season, there is no real collaborative dimension apart from common publicity. An example of a *pseudo-consortium*, driven by the common quest for visibility and a limited synergy in PR.

Recently, 19 national cultural agencies formed the European Union National Institutes for Culture (EUNIC) in order to seed networks and stimulate consortia forming. It remains to be seen whether cooperation instigated on the level of national directorates will be more successful than the cooperation efforts undertaken locally.

The formation of consortia among some prominent European museums, often in conjunction with their US counterparts, undertaken for the preparation, production and touring of large, extremely expensive blockbuster exhibitions might create jealousy and disappointment among certain other museums which feel snubbed and left out. In cultural heritage, the formation of international consortia is habitual, in order to pool resources and know-how in delicate and complex restoration projects.

Despite all the tensions, contradictory developments and changes in the evolution of individual consortiums, the model in itself indicates a certain stabilization of international cultural cooperation and the emergence of some strong, ambitious players in all disciplines who seek prolonged forms of multilateral engagement with the pooling of resources and sharing of risks. The crucial role of networks in seeding the consortia is not always sufficiently recognized, either by the consortia members or by the subsidy givers. That with the emergence of more sophisticated forms of international cultural cooperation networks have become superfluous is not the case at all; on the contrary, they have become even more important to ensure the inflow of new generations of cultural operators, provide them with an international context, equip them with information, insights and competences and stimulate them to seek and articulate their own advanced forms of international cooperation.

11

STRATEGIC ISSUES

This last chapter addresses some strategic issues that demand the unwavering attention of an internationally operating cultural professional. As interrelated international projects create a certain pattern, strategic considerations and choices need to underly all the work. They concern the operator's position, sense of priorities, key relationships, a set of permeating values, an understanding of shifts in particular national cultural systems and cultural conditions in Europe, and finally a notion of one's own operational territory, especially in relation to the political and cultural pressures of economic globalization.

Sustainability, autonomy, continuity

Most professionals working in non-profit cultural organizations experience their position as fragile, vulnerable and much dependent on the public subsidies for culture that are in most European countries stagnating or shrinking. Even publicly endowed institutions which receive regular subsidies from public authorities sometimes, almost automatically, react anxiously to competition from the cultural industry and worry about the rising costs of their operation. They resent politics when it flip-flops on promises and issues, pursues representational and programing goals alone and treats contemporary creativity and cultural heritage as a *creative industry* rather than as unique and distinct domains of cultural production and distribution. Even worse, when politics imposes operating standards proper to business, pressures cultural organizations to earn a growing percentage of their own budget and to fundraise from other sources. Cultural operators try to live with these contingencies, but often experience them as destabilizing. *Sustainability* of most non-profit cultural institutions is an issue, a concern, not a self-evident prospect. Many cultural initiatives never reach the stage where they can constitute themselves as a separate legal entity, as a non-profit organization. Those who succeed often disappear within a few years of functioning due to lack of funds, debts or uncertain subsidy prospects. Relatively few organizations make the transition to some sort of structural public funding and hardly any transform from the non-profit to a for-profit status. In addition, mergers and reorganizations reshuffle the cultural field, often driven by politicians who seek to *rationalize* their functioning and to economize on subsidy.

In such charged circumstances international cultural cooperation appears as a *strategic orientation* to enhance sustainability and provide the organization with some *midrange continuity*. Cross border partnerships are developed in order to supplement existing resources, build additional competences and open the way to extended distribution outlets. International cooperation is thus part of the function of institutional development. In practice, however, mistakes made in the choice of partners and in managing the partner relationships and projects could affect the sustainability of the organization, weaken it and expose it to additional media critique, political pressure and economic hardships.

Some cultural operators define themselves as an *independent* artist, *independent* programmer, *independent* curator, *independent* producer, *independent* manager, trying to say that they are self-employed, work freelance or for a small organization or association that has no steady subsidy but survives from project to project. In such working conditions this insistence on independence is quite self-deceiving. Better to acknowledge vulnerability, the discontinuity of engagement and *dependencies* one has. All these self-labeled independent professionals depend on their colleagues, peer organizations, private and public subsidies, contracts, commissions, competitions, clients, sponsors, patrons, markets, media and ultimately audiences. It is not a false independence that should be emphasized but rather a sense of *autonomy*.

Autonomy is a more relative and elastic notion that does not exclude the dependences of a cultural professional and yet accommodates all the strong motivations, the desire to be original, unique, freedom in setting one's priorities and articulating one's values. For an individual professional, especially a self-employed one or a freelancer, autonomy implies a certain freedom in choosing partners, patrons, clients and financiers in accordance with the cultural or artistic project and ambitions they have, and the entitlement to realize it in tune with their own imagination, talent, inspiration and competence. Most commonly, within some agreed upon terms and conditions, and perhaps with some basic socioeconomic provisions derived from the acknowledged professional status. Autonomy is relationally defined, it creates a relative zone of freedom within the framework set up by the relationship and therefore an *autonomous artist* recognizes the web of their own professional relationships while a so-called or self-declared *independent artist* seeks to deny them or pretends that they do not matter.

Even in a small cultural organization, autonomy is shaped first of all as the quality of relationship between the board and the executive/management, and between the latter and the staff, as a delicate set of agreements, concordance, mutual respect that structure the programmatic framework in a recognizable way but without imposition and de-motivating restraints. This sense of autonomy could be articulated only if:

- the organization has a clear mission and structure,

- prerogatives of the executive/management are clearly defined,

- staff is recruited on the basis of job descriptions and

- members of the board develop a professional attitude to their role, profile it as a public task and not as a surveillance duty, personal hobby or a friendly service to the executive/management.

International cooperation needs to be integrated in this framework of agreements, roles and responsibilities—not as a luxury, ornament or incident, but as an *organic* aspect of the organization. Otherwise, those who work on international tasks and projects will not be able to assert their own operational autonomy, without which they cannot expect to be successful.

In the external sense, autonomy qualifies primarily the relationship of the cultural organization with its financiers, both public and private. Autonomy denotes the conditions under which external subsidies, grants, sponsorships, donations are given, and the expectations and appointments that the organization has to deliver in return. For institutions that do not enjoy a certain degree of operational autonomy, it is practically impossible to engage in international cultural cooperation, except perhaps in the most rudimentary forms, such as those pre-arranged or imposed exchange schemes, described in chapter 4. Without a sufficient degree of autonomy, a cultural organization cannot operate in the international field, develop ideas, find partners, work with them and realize projects. Even if such international practice is made possible, the organization engaged and financiers might find each other at cross purposes: the organization does it out of artistic ambition, cultural exploration and developmental trust, while financiers expect more promotion and prestige export.

Furthermore, a cultural organization working internationally might be primarily interested in exploring collaborative and creative processes while the financier is perhaps focused on the immediate and visible results. Professionals care about the quality and dynamics of the collaborative relationship among participants while a financier is interested primarily in the effects achieved on the public, the media echo, which can again be computed as a prestige score in the international arena.

Disputes about the desirable degree of autonomy could disrupt the continuity of a cultural organization or at least the continuity of its international engagement. Financiers may reduce the subsidy, demand a discontinuation of international programs, force the executive out or de-fund the organization and force it into liquidation. Especially publicly funded organizations operate in this danger zone, and might be affected by a change of ruling politicians, parties and majorities. A sharp reduction in an organization's subsidy, for instance, could make international cooperation impossible for a while. If some key professionals leave, insights, skills, know-how and networks will also be lost to this institution and will have to be rebuilt from scratch, if and when international engagement becomes possible once more.

With private financiers, such as foundations, continuity is also problematic, since they tend to give single grants or grants that are renewable once or twice and then move to other clients and opportunities. An organization working internationally, especially if it is largely or exclusively dependent on project grants, public or private, needs to calculate and allocate some resources needed for prospecting and fundraising in order to have a new grant available when one project is terminated and another one is ready to begin. If a small cultural organization is completely immersed in the realization of an ongoing project and omits to seek funds for a future one in time, it might come into a dangerous situation, slip into a crisis, even liquidation. Discontinuity might emerge as a threat even if the organization has been successful with the previous project, but is utterly exhausted from it, because it takes quite a bit of time to set up a new project and find and receive funds for its realization.

Values and ethics

Those cultural operators who often and intensively work on an international scale are sometimes asked whether they feel more loyalty to domestic or foreign partners and audiences. This is only seemingly an opposition: most professionals need both: domestic for familiarity, reassurance and intimacy;

foreign for the challenge, surprise and inspiration. The opposition of loyalties to artists and professional peers vs. loyalty to audiences is equally artificial. A professional thrives in a professional context and thus needs the nurturing relations with peers in order to create value for the audiences. Arrogant disregard of the audience or pandering to the public erodes the professional respect and reputation of a professional among colleagues. There are professionals who work more with artists than with audiences directly, as for instance someone who runs workshops for artists or a residency program; what matters in all relationships, with professional colleagues and with the audience, is how much those relationships have been shaped by *integrity* and an internalized set of values. Without them, professionalism and artistic excellence have little sense.

The question of values appears in international cultural cooperation in a perhaps more charged and accented manner than in local work, because international engagements demand additional effort, resources, energy and a high degree of intercultural competence. Furthermore, despite our presumed common European traits, some values are culturally constructed or colored and could be unrecognized or misinterpreted. In complex multilateral projects flexibility, self-discipline and understanding of the position and objectives of others comes up as a critical value and not just a skill. Deception, arrogance, selfishness and self-promotion ruin the personal trust without which international projects cannot work.

Beside personal issues, there are specific *institutional issues*. Cooperating partners working together may quite vary in size, economic power, prestige and position in their own domestic cultural system. This difference should not be interpreted as a license for institutional arrogance, dominance and exploitative attitude. Fairness and equality need to be seen as a stepping stone of international cooperation even—or rather: *especially* if partners do not/cannot invest the same resources in the projects. The sense of *parity* and shared responsibility should be nurtured above differences in economic power or accumulated reputation and prestige. All cultural operators are, in a way, products of their own cultural system, through education, practice and implicit and sometimes unconscious cultural grooming. There is a possibility therefore that they believe that the way of doing things they are used to at home is also the best or only way of operating internationally. Stubborn insistence to operate internationally and especially abroad, as if they were at home, betrays an ignorance of the prevailing differences among cultural systems in Europe and could alienate partners and torpedo the project. To insist that only *our way* of working together is professional and other ways are not is culturally insensitive. To use economic superiority to embarrass or humiliate partners is even worse.

⌘   Colleagues from the former DDR tell of the *Wessies* who, after German reunification, went from the West to East Germany to teach their new fellow countrymen modern cultural management, production and marketing, and displayed vanity, arrogance and unbearable paternalism. That they were sometimes not the very best professionals, but those who could not prosper in the former West Germany, and now went East for very high salaries as miracle makers, made things only worse. If such irritations could be felt among *Wessies* and *Ossies*, divided for 45 years by the Cold War, one could imagine the irritation some Western European colleagues caused in enthusiastic but often culturally insensitive cooperation with peers from the former communist countries, many of whom learned how to survive and to create subterfuges under bureaucratic harassment and censorship the hard way, in communist times.

⌘   Another affront comes from a steady stream of mediocre trainers and aggressive consultants descending from Western Europe on the cultural infrastructure of former communist countries in Central and Eastern Europe to peddle the gospel of *creative industry* and *cultural tourism*, *sponsorship* and *marketing*, often in ignorance of the cultural conditions under the former communist system, its inheritance and the turbulent socio-economic transition that ensued after 1989. Their proscriptive know-how, perhaps successful at home, can not always fit the circumstances and the needs they fail to grasp. An English arts and culture consultancy, skillful in working with municipalities and cultural organization in its domestic market but completely ignorant of the recent history and transition tribulations of the post-Communist Baltic countries, can strive to market its services aggressively in Riga or Vilnius, but will have to undergo a considerable learning period, paid by its local client, before it can deliver any know-how.

Culture professionals in Southeastern Europe, in Turkey and Caucasus complain sometimes of the *pathology* of *donor driven* cooperation and the limitations forthcoming from their donor dependence. Where there is hardly any local money to enable domestic cultural operators to work internationally, they depend on foreign embassies and foreign cultural agencies, foreign NGOs and foundations active in their territory and often encounter the kind of arrogance and indifference that they are used to meeting when dealing with their own government bureaucracy.

⌘ Colleagues in Bosnia Herzegovina and Kosovo, for instance, complain of donors who condition, limit, restrict and steer the project proposal to match their own expectations, fabricate an appearance of multicultural cooperation where it does not really exist or impose foreign partners from their own country, regardless of the match with the local operators.

Donors' attention to a certain region is very much conditioned by political developments and opportunities. New focal points of crises pull donors from one area to another, from Bosnia to Kosovo and from there to Georgia or Azerbaijan. Structures, capacities, projects and programs get abandoned in haste, expectations created remain unfulfilled, contacts made are allowed to disappear, and partnerships to collapse.

⌘ Since 1993, the Paris magazine *Transeuropéennes* dedicated a lot of attention to the cultural dimension and consequences of the wars in former Yugoslavia, but developed in parallel, a web of summer courses, workshops, conferences and seminars for graduate students, academics, artists and intellectuals from Southeastern Europe, which took place in the region and in France. The initial impulse was to provide some antidote for the nationalist and xenophobic propaganda of the media and much of the academia; later the emphasis came to lie on civil society development, modernization of universities and academic ethics, autonomous media and cultural activities, with the participation of partners from several European countries and those in the region, encompassing some 12 states, from Slovenia to Turkey and Cyprus. A considerable network emerged whose members and activities fed the content of the magazine. Sometime around 2002 the Balkans, or rather South Eastern Europe seemingly went out of fashion among donors, and it became increasingly difficult to raise governmental or foundation grants for the new projects. In 2003 *Transeuropéennes* stopped publishing and its network disintegrated.

Despite an advanced degree of European integration, many European people have traumatic memories, turbulent historic remembrances and problematic relations with other countries and nations, usually in their neighborhood, or with some of their ethnic minorities and majorities. An ignorant cultural operator might come into a situation abroad, to do or say something offensive, unaware of the surrounding emotional minefield, offending inadvertently.

⌘ Simple ignorance could also be interpreted as arrogance. Those who have a flakey geographic knowledge, who tend to confuse Slovenia and Slovakia, Budapest and Bucharest, Plzen and Poznan better be warned—before they embark on international cultural cooperation!

While international cultural cooperation could be seen as an efficient vehicle to counter ignorance, stereotypes and prejudices many in Europe still nourish about their fellow Europeans (and especially about immigrants of non-European origin), it is sometimes abused and appropriated by zealous patriots who in their passionate championship of their own national culture easily slide into nationalism and even chauvinism, and parade their own absolute historic truth through contentious historic narratives that still prevail among the people of Europe. Projects that reconsider cultural layers of truncated mythologies and fabricated traditions critically can nurture trust, mutual interest and deliver cultural and artistic *confidence building measures* against exclusivist claims and one-sided interpretations.

⌘ Fondacja zagranyczna (Borderland Foundation) in Szejne, in the northeastern part of Poland, has been exploring the common history and intercultural connections among inhabitants in that particular triangle of Poland, Byelorussia and Lithuania for years. Located in a former synagogue, Borderland also keeps alive the memory of Jewish presence in this region, eradicated in the Holocaust. The programs are practically all border-crossing, focused on artists, educators and students in the region, with frequent guests from elsewhere.

There is much attention paid to *visibility* in international cultural cooperation. This is, normal to an extent, because both operators and financiers want to make sure that what they do in the international arena at the cost of considerable effort and resources, is properly registered and appreciated both at home and abroad. But this emphasis on visibility needs to be matched with sufficient attention to *transparency* and *accountability,* and that covers openness about objectives, partners, investments, expenses, finances, results and overall impact of the projects carried out and completed. In recent years, there has been increasing sensitivity on the part of public authorities, from any small municipality up to the European Commission, for transparency and accountability in the way they use taxpayer's money and what effects they achieve. Similarly, there are stricter rules about reporting and accounts of business companies, especially those that operate internationally, prompted largely by huge scandals and abuse. Surprisingly, this increased scrutiny of government expenditure and corporate operations has not lead to much reconsideration of the quality of *governance* in the cultural systems so far, and this includes public and private institutions, foundations and cultural associations and the way their boards fulfill their tasks. Large business companies not only have to conform to the accountancy criteria set by the European Commission, but beside their business practices and outcomes they must increasingly address the social and environmental aspects of their work in their annual reports (*PPP = profit, people, planet*).

In the world of culture there is a great deal of divergence with regard to how organizations, their leaders and their boards understand their own legal and moral obligation to report on their activities, what they disclose and how they explain it. International projects need extra explaining in annual reports, because they are often realized far away from the domestic public attention, they have a different structure of expenditure than domestic projects, use considerable amounts of money, sometimes for very intensive and short-lasting activities. Cultural institutions usually lack clear policies for how they distribute their annual report and how they ensure sufficient transparency in their web sites, newsletters and brochures. Subsidy givers rarely require their recipients to respect some *transparency standards*. Those who decide on the subsidies for cultural organizations are in most cases not really in a position to assess the effectiveness of the activities carried out abroad because they have not been around. And most public subsidy givers in many countries could considerably improve their own procedures, criteria and argumentation in allocating subsidy for some special international projects and abandon the practice of *special* and *discretionary funds* deployed for special cultural events and otherwise unknown and inaccessible for normal applications. With increased pressure on cultural organizations to generate their own income, it is important to clearly explain in reports, the source and structure of that income, and offer convincing assurances that the generation of its own income does not alter the not-for-profit status of the organization, that the income has been reinvested in core activities.

Cultural dimension
of European integration

The present dynamic and intensity of international cultural cooperation in Europe can be seen as a positive outcome of the end of the Cold War and the tempo of European integration. Future perspectives are equally dependent on the further course and speed of European integration, especially after the fiasco of the proposed European Constitution and deep divisions expressed about EU budgetary priorities, further enlargement with new members states and common policies in some sensitive areas, including security, judiciary, and market liberalization. Culture and international cultural cooperation enjoy a limited embedding in the EU institutional mechanism. Even the formulation in the draft Constitution (2004), based on article 151 of the Treaty of Nice, defined culture only as a *shared competence* between the EU and national governments, but it at least intended to replace unanimous decision making in cultural matters with the qualified majority vote. There are many politicians who argue that the EU should do less in order to do better, and that certain policy domains—culture, for instance—should be renationalized, because of the *democratic deficit* in EU functioning and because the bureaucratic maneuvers and oblique procedures remain ungraspable for the ordinary people and make them indifferent or hostile to the EU.

Despite this steady resistance of various Eurosceptics, in May 2007 the Euroepan Commission published its "Communication" on culture, setting out its priorities for the next few years. The focus is on *cultural diversity* and *intercultural dialogue*, connecting the citizens in Europe; the notion of *creativity*, tied to the EU Lisbon Agenda and thus to economic growth, knowledge-based economy and more and better jobs; and on the *cultural dimension* of the EU foreign and security policy.

As much as globalization and migratory pressures create some anxieties, additionally accented by the institutional impasse in which the EU found itself in 2005, a certain nostalgia for the protective shield and supposed democratic accountability of the national state cannot provide appropriate response for most of the challenges facing Europe and the world. Culture might seem a marginal issue to many in comparison with environmental protection, energy supply, public health and epidemic prevention, security, airspace control, fundamental research ...—all those mighty domains that clearly demand European rather than national solutions. Cultural systems *are* and *remain* in the competence of national governments and increasingly of regions and municipalities, but cultural industry has in the meantime become truly global. It is the international cultural *cooperation platforms and instruments*, not cultural *production and distribution* as such, that require an intensified EU investment, because all other levels of public authority, and especially national governments tend to invest in this domain predominantly in a bilateral logic and driven by their own promotional objectives.

An EU commitment to international cultural cooperation, expressed in an improved and more specific cultural program, with an increased budget in relation to the one secured for 2007-2013, would help—together with all other public and private input—reduce the disparities and investment capacities between the rich and relatively poor countries and cultural systems, big and small cultural markets, demographically homogenous and heterogeneous countries, much and less affected by migration, those belonging to some large linguistic systems (English, French, Spanish) and those that are linguistically small and isolated.

Compared to EU structural funds for harmonization of regional socioeconomic conditions, the investment in international cultural cooperation should be seen as one of the key solidarity measures, but it is more than *800 times smaller* in resources deployed (euro 336 billion vs 408 million for 2007-2013). This tiny investment seeks to shape Europe as an inclusive and dynamic cultural space that nurtures creativity and cultural participation, stimulates intercultural curiosity and competence across the boundaries of the national states, national cultural systems, languages and traditions and enhances the sense of European citizenship. The frequently invoked diversity of European cultures is to be reasserted against the uniformizing pressures of globalized cultural industry, and not in a self-enclosure, or protectionist defense of frozen identities, but in more intensive international cultural cooperation that creates shared experiences and shared values and aspirations, mutual respect, sense of proximity and trust among the citizens of Europe.

The priority expenditures of the EU in this domain should be: the international *networks* as the primary infrastructure of international cultural cooperation; *mobility* schemes and Europe wide *information, documentation* and *training* programs; *short term* experimental and complex *prolonged* multilateral consortia and their projects; and especially programs and projects engaging European creativity with counterparts *outside* Europe. The EU global position and external policies with regard to third countries and other world's regions need to be enriched with a strong *cultural dimension*, commensurate to the richness of traditions and the development level of cultural infrastructure in Europe. National governments, together with regions and municipalities, should invest in interfaces and facilitators of international cultural cooperation rather than in promotional agencies and anachronistic and wasteful institutions preoccupied with the exportation of prestige. International appreciation of a nation's own cultural richness and specific values is best shaped through a generous provision of hospitality, schemes that offer residences, meeting opportunities and workshops to cultural operators from abroad, matched with provisions enabling local talent to go abroad and work with their peers.

European and global

In today's globalized and instantaneous world, and especially in much of Europe, as one integrated market, the firm boundaries between domestic and international cultural engagement make little sense. In fact, the major challenge of cultural operators today is to draw upon a maximum synergy of their local and international work, to go beyond a simple balancing act and fuse, integrate and mutually enrich those dimensions, to create cultural value that is inspired by locality but strives to involve talents from elsewhere and reach out to distant audiences. With multilateral cooperative projects, programs are created not for here *or* there but for *here, there and elsewhere*. But there is a certain danger of dissipation of energy, loss of focus and a sense of place, confusion of priorities and enmeshment of localities.

In sorting out priorities of engagement, first attention should be given to one's neighbors, to the potential partners just across the national borders, as Fondacyja zagranyczna has been doing, where there is shared proximity as much as conflict and tension, where *narcissism of small differences* could manifest itself and reinforce separation and suspicion, as has been the case in the Balkans throughout the 1990s.

⌘ Balkan Express is an emerging network of artists, producers and presenters reaching across boundaries in a region that suffers from a *surplus of history* and still has not recovered from recent mass destruction, war crimes, collapse of established cultural links and ensuing isolation. The network strives to nurture multilateral creative consortia and provide mobility of talents and distribution of cultural goods, thus restoring a sense of neighborhood and surpassing hatred and prejudice.

Another priority is cultural engagement with the countries from which *mass migration* to Europe has originated, as an integral part of the integration policy. To understand immigrant cultures and facilitate their connectivity with the cultural system of the recipient country both traditional and contemporary culture, cultural heritage and contemporary creativity need to be invoked and explored. Many immigrants in Europe and their descendents are ignorant of the contemporary culture of their country of origin, while Europeans nurture simplistic *folkloric* notions of those countries, shaped by mass tourism and shopping expeditions to pitoresque bazaars.

⌘   Istanbul Arts and Culture Foundation (IKSV) has been organizing large programs of contemporary Turkish culture in Stuttgart, Berlin and other European cities where large Turkish migrant communities live, seeking to present them in the mainstream cultural facilities and in cooperation with major media, and thus overcome the almost automatic marginalization of Turkish culture to peripheral, ethnic, ghetto circuits, reaching the core cultural public and the Turkish migrants.

The third priority is an orchestrated European engagement with cultures in the *EU's immediate neighborhood,* especially with the countries of the Southern Mediterranean where contemporary cultural production often suffers from poverty and corruption, governmental repression and censorship, and parallely from the hostility of fanatic religionists. Instead of competing actions of national cultural agencies and cultural attaches in the Arab world the EU should, as part of its own foreign policy and revived *Barcelona process,* encourage multilateral partnerships and consider setting up *houses of European cultures* in key cities of the region, staffed by experienced cultural operators rather than diplomats. These cultural centers would explore the parameters of cultures in Europe in interaction with the local operators and in accordance with local circumstances, needs, and creative resources. And how about an *internship* scheme for European students and starting cultural professionals, to be absorbed for 3-6 months in those centers? And a generous European *visitors* program, whereby local artists and intellectuals would travel for a study visit to several EU countries in one trip, and if invited to a conference in Barcelona, have a chance to give a workshop in Lisbon or attend a seminar in Lyon?

International cultural cooperation with *distant non-European* countries is more expensive and more complicated, especially if those countries lack a cultural infrastructure compatible with that of Europe, and if their governments see culture only as a supplement to the tourism industry and not as a developmental right of their people. A successful cultural operator exploring European perimeters will certainly very soon consider engagements in North America or Australia, New Zeeland, Japan and Singapore. There are also examples of international cultural cooperation, initiated from Europe, being integrated with the development cooperation and supported partially by its governmental and intergovernmental agencies and resources in Uganda, Guinea, Peru... Inevitably, emerging superpowers such as China, India, Brazil and South Africa appear as new challenges and targets, especially for the more experienced European cultural operators, seasoned previously in a series of Europe-focused projects.

The contribution of international cultural cooperation to emerging European citizenship should be seen only as a stepping stone for the cultural grounding of a *global citizenship*, with global awareness, responsibility and sense of solidarity. With the geographic and cultural borders of Europe eluding any specific definition, this handbook inevitably ends with an encouragement to keep probing and transcending the concentric circles surrounding one's own home territory, and to continue further and further. International cultural cooperation cannot be imagined nor implemented outside the political and economic context of globalization. Yet critical stances towards globalization and its capacity to redistribute and monopolize power, wealth and opportunities at the expense of justice and equality rest on an appreciation of cultural diversity and sense of cultural solidarity, affirmed by various forms of international cultural cooperation.

KEY WORDS

This small glossary has no encyclopedic or lexicographic ambitions. It contains a limited number of terms frequently used in this handbook and describes the meaning the author attaches to them. Since this handbook will presumably be used also by readers who are not native speakers of English, the inclusion of a glossary seeks to avoid misunderstandings and confusion with similar words that might, in some European languages, have a different common meaning.

access: opportunity and capacity to take advantage of some resource, entitlement to apply for a certain subsidy or possibility to take part in cultural life, to be included and considered as a player, factor or audience.

advocacy: advancement of some public, non-commercial interest by a specific group or sector and its agents (education, arts and culture, public health, environment, etc.) in the public opinion, bringing forth ideas, arguments and policy proposals, targeting decision makers, media and figures and institutions of influence. Opp. to **lobbying** that seeks to influence public opinion and decision making for the benefit of some commercial interests, such as tobacco, alcohol, construction industry or airlines.

alternative culture: different in relation to the dominant, prevailing, mainstream cultural constellation.

audience development: conscious and systematic effort to create, enlarge and upgrade or change the audience, stimulate and nurture through programming and a variety of supporting activities of promotional and educational nature the emergence of a knowledgeable and demanding audience.

autonomy: relative distance of an individual, a body or an organization from a source of power and influence, based on an agreement of mutual responsibilities and trust, as in the autonomy of a cultural organization from the subsidy giver and of an executive from the board.

arms' length: a symbolic measure of desired distance between public authorities and cultural operators that is intended to ensure some respect for the autonomy of the latter. Also a distance between the political power that makes public resources available and those who decide about detailed policy and their concrete allocation.

community: a slightly romantic notion of a group of people united by some micro territory or some common origin, descent, ethnicity, language, religion, culture, etc. Implies conformity and harmony rather than difference and dissent, stability rather than dynamism.

co-production: a formal arrangement of two or more parties to create jointly some new work through sharing of investment, organizational capacity, management and logistic provisions.

creative industries: much used British oxymoron seeking to make contemporary creativity more respectable by calling it an industry, analogous to the hospitality industry and tourist industry. Fuses or mixes up the profit seeking industry and non-profit creativity, which is in its methods of production, not industrial at all.

crossover: work crossing the boundaries between specific artistic disciplines.

cultural democracy: a constellation of equality in entitlement and empowerment to participate in cultural expression and utilization of the available cultural resources (a 'bottom up' dynamic).

cultural diversity: often argued, in analogy with biodiversity, as a value on its own, emanating from the parallel existence of a multitude of cultural expressions that deserve protection and stimulation. Seen as a counterpart to the uniformizing impact of the cultural industry that threatens cultural diversity. Subject of a 2005 UNESCO's *Convention on the Protection and Promotion of the Diversity of Cultural Expressions*. The term entered the usage in order to replace so-called *cultural exception*, which claims that cultural goods are not like ordinary economic goods and therefore deserve special protection. Chiefly used to defend a regime of protection, privilege and subsidy of national and/or EU audiovisual industry against global competition.

cultural heritage: cultural goods inherited from the past, whether material or immaterial, influencing cultural memory. Subject to special protection regimes, standards and the UNESCO and Council of Europe conventions as well as elaborate national legislation.

cultural industry: used originally by T. Adorno & M. Horkheimer (*Kulturindustrie*) to describe an industrial method in the production of cultural meaning, image and symbols, originally applied to publishing, advertising, film and radio. Later extended to cover television and fashion and the entire range of digital cultural products.

cultural rights: a special branch of human rights, related to the cultural expression of groups and individuals and their access to cultural goods, including certain protection measures benefiting minorities.

curator: person charged with the task of conceptualizing an exhibition and selecting the works for it, determines their display and comments on them, thus serving as an intermediary between the artists and the public.

decentralization: a movement to shift responsibility for some domain (for instance, culture) from the national government to the regional and local authorities.

distribution: system of measures and facilities ensuring that cultural goods reach a public.

dialogue of cultures: refers vaguely to the desirability of the intercultural dialogue and of a climate of respect, tolerance and understanding among various cultures, religions and ideological orientations. European Union has declared 2008 a Year of Intercultural Dialogue.

employability: capacities and resources which will make one employable, make it more likely that a person will find a job.

executive producer: management function of a person in charge of the production process and responsible for all its aspects, elements and collaborators. Used in the performing arts, film, sometimes also for complex exhibitions, conferences and other events with much logistic complexity.

festival: an intensive program of cultural and artistic events, packaged in a thematic or disciplinary formula and offered in a compact time sequence, and usually located within a specified venue, borough, town, city or geographical area.

foundation: a non-profit organization with a beneficial fiscal status, set up by individuals, corporations, public authorities and others, usually in order to realize its stated purpose. If it has some initial capital (endowment) or a regular inflow of means from the founder, it could function as a grant-giving foundation; if it seeks to raise funds from other sources for its own activities, it is an operating foundation.

globalization: interdependence and accellerated and intensified interactivity of production and distribution of goods, images, ideas, styles and habits worldwide. Refers to the movement of people, goods and symbolic meanings.

governance: the responsibility and the quality of the main legally responsible decision making or supervisory body in a political and territorial organization, in business corporations and in non-profit organizations.

institutional fatigue: institutions becoming dysfunctional because they are loaded with routine, paralyzed by problems they cannot resolve, mainly emanating from their type or model that has become inadequate or anachronistic.

interculturalism: interaction of cultural groups despite and across their differences.

inter-disciplinary: a quality emanating from the fusion of various (artistic) disciplines.

mainstreaming: shifting some ideas, values, or products from the margins of society and alternative realms of culture into the center of public attention.

matching funds: funds granted in certain proportion (for instance 1:1 or 1:2) to those who already have found some resources elsewhere.

multiculturalism: coexistence of various cultures in the same place; also a policy of managing cultural differences and competing interests of cultural groupings.

new media: refers to all sorts of emerging digital platforms.

NGO: non-governmental organization, set up for some non-commercial purpose: political, cultural, social, educational, sportive...

non-profit: operating for public benefit, i.e. not for the purpose of creating profit for founders or nominal owners, who are thus obliged to reinvest all possible gains in the operation.

peer review: assessment of an individual, collective or institutional performance by the colleagues who are assumed to posses the same or comparable expertise as those being assessed.

pilot project: a project limited in time and scope, run as an experiment in order to test a certain practice, procedure or mode of operation before it is applied more broadly and regularly.

presenter-programmer: offers the public a certain cultural and artistic program on the basis of own expertise, insight, network, personal choice and available budgets.

private-public partnership: joint investment and/or operational responsibility of the private (often corporate) side and a governmental body.

project funding: limited funds, made available to carry out a specific project rather than to enable the functioning of some organization (opp. to revenue, 'current', institutional or structural funding).

public space: physical and symbolic place, free for the public to access and thus entitled to some protection of freedom of expression; and yet at the same time subject to some restrictions for the sake of public safety (maximum legal occupancy, quality of air standards, noise-level restrictions, fire prevention measures).

QUANGO: quasi-non-govermental organization. An organization that appears autonomous from the government but is in fact a publicly funded and directed agency, albeit operating at some distance from government itself.

regionalization: endowing some regions with political competence as part of a political decentralisation process.

site-specific: an art work or event created in a concrete space on the basis of its specific parameters and qualities.

social cohesion: intensity and quality of social interactions among groups and individuals in a given territory, trust they share and their presumed readiness for collaboration.

social exclusion: deprivation of some social groups through legal measures or social practices, discrimination resulting in social marginality.

sponsorship: a transaction whereby a commercial organization gives, under conditions specified in detail, means or services in kind to a non-profit organization in order to benefit from the association with it and its cultural, educational, social, artistic or sport prestige and reputation and earn the appreciation of the public.

stakeholder: individuals, interest groups, corporations and organizations affected by or capable of affecting a policy, a programme, an organization, or a project. Opp. to **shareholder** which denotes economic co-ownership rather than a position of influence.

structural funding: long term funding of an organization; even if the volume might vary from year to year, the assumption made is that the organization is entitled to continued funding. Not to be confused with the structural funds of the EU, directed at the harmonization of socioeconomic conditions of population, a solidarity measure aiding less developed regions.

subsidiarity: a principle much invoked in the EU, stipulating that each competence should exist at the lowest possible level of decision-making where it can be properly executed. If national government can do something well, the European Commission should not be in charge, but if it can be done better by the regional or local authorities, the national government should pass the responsibility down to whichever level is most appropriate.

third sector: a vague notion lumping together all organizations that are neither government nor business, thus all not-for-profit organizations, associations, foundations, volunteers, etc.

transition: a vague description of the ongoing process in Central and Eastern Europe, from communism to capitalism, from one-party dictatorship to multi-party parliamentary democracy, from planned to market economy, from censored but lavishly subsidized cultural production to a cultural infrastructure ailing in scarcity and indifference, sinking into commercialism and trivia.

urban cultures: plurality of cultural expressions emerging in contemporary urban agglomerations, esp. those marked by the coexistence and interaction of different cultural groups and much affected by migration.

volunteers: persons who work a certain number of hours regularly on certain precisely defined tasks without being paid for their time and effort, because they do it for their own pleasure or out of a sense of service to the public. Much used practice in non-profit world and esp. in culture, to substitute for staff functions that are not covered by the means available.

KEY PLAYERS

This is a selective list of international networks and organizations in Europe and of cultural institutions and programs that have a pronounced international character.

Adam Mickiewicz Institute — www.iam.pl
AEC (Association Européenne des Consérvatoires) — www.aecinfo.org
AEC (Associazione per l'economia della cultura)
    — www.economiadellacultura.it
AFO (Association Française des Orchestres) — www.france-orchestres.com
Akademie der Künste (Berlin) — www.adk.de
Alexander S. Onassis Public Benefit Foundation — www.onassis.gr
Alliance Française — www.alliancefr.org
Allianz KulturStiftung — www.allianz-kulturstiftung.de
Anna Lindh Euro-Mediterranean Foundation for the Dialogue Between Cultures
    — http://europa.eu.int/comm/external_relations/euromed/euromed_foundation/
    and — www.euromedalex.org/En/AboutUs.htm
Archa Theatre (Prague) — www.archatheatre.cz
Ars Baltica — www.ars-baltica.net
Ars Electronica (Linz) — www.aec.at
ArtFactories — www.artfactories.net
Arts Council England — www.artscouncil.org.uk
Arts Council of Ireland — www.artscouncil.ie
Arts Wales — www.artswales.org.uk
ArtServis — www.artservis.org
ASEF (Asia-Europe Foundation) — www.asef.org
ASSITEJ (Association International du Theatre pour l'enfance et la jeunesse)
    — www.assitej.org

Balkankult — www.balkankult.org

Batory Foundation — www.batory.org.pl

BOCCF (Bank of Cyprus Cultural Foundation)
— www.boccf.org/main/ default.aspx

Bertelsmann Stiftung — www.bertelsmann-stiftung.de

BJCEM (Biennale des Jeunes Créateurs d'Europe et de la Méditerranée)
— www.biennalegiovani.org

Boekman Stichting — www.boekman.nl

Borderland Foundation — www.pogranicze.sejny.pl

British Council — www.britishcouncil.org

Budapest Observatory — www.budobs.org

C³ Center for Culture & Communication — www.c3.hu/c3/index.html

Calouste Gulbenkian Foundation UK — www.gulbenkian.org.uk

Carpathian Foundation — www.carpathianfoundaton.org

Caucasus Foundation — www.caucasusfoundation.ge

CCP Austria — http://www.ccp-austria.at

CCP Belgium (Flemish Community) — www.culturenet.be

CCP Belgium (French and German Community) — www.pcceurope.be

CCP Czech Republic — www.culture2000.cz
and — www.supp.cz/html/culture2000heritage

CCP Denmark — www.kunststyrelsen.dk

CCP Estonia — www.ccp.einst.ee

CCP Finland — www.cimo.fi

CCP France (Relais Culture Europe) — www.relais-culture-europe.org/

CCP Germany — www.ccp-deutschland.de/

CCP Greece — www.ccp.culture.gr

CCP Hungary — www.kulturpont.hu

CCP Iceland — www.evropumenning.is and — www.artscouncil.ie
and — www.ccp.ie

CCP Italy — www.antennaculturale.it

CCP Lithuania — www.durys.org

CCP Luxembourg — www.gouvernement.lu/gouv/fr/doss/rce

CCP Malta — www.culture.org.mt

CCP Norway — www.kulturrad.no

CCP Poland — www.mk.gov.pl/pkk

CCP Portugal — http://cultura2000.min-cultura.pt

CCP Cyprus — www.moec.gov.cy/ccp/index.html

CCP Romania — www.cultura2000.ro

CCP Slovakia — www.ccp.sk

CCP Slovenia (SCCA) — www.scca-ljubljana.si/ccp
CCP Spain — www.mcu.es/cooperacion/pcc/index.html
CCP Sweden — www.kulturradet.se and http://www.raa.se
CCP the Netherlands (SICA) www.sica.nl
CCP UK (Euclide) — www.euclid.info/uk/index.htm
    and — www.euclid.info/uk/Culture2000
CCP Latvia — www.km.gov.lv/kultura2000
CCP Bulgaria — www.mct.government.bg and — www.eubcc.bg
CCPs (Cultural Contact Points)
    — http://europa.eu.int/comm/culture/eac/ culture2000/contacts/national_
    pts_en.html
CCR (Cultural Centers – Historic Monuments) — www.accr-europe.org
CDRSEE (Center for Democracy and Reconciliation in Southeast Europe)
    — www.cdrsee.org
Center for Cultural Decontamination (Belgrade) — www.czkd.org.yu
Central and Eastern Europe's Cultural Institutions — www.cee-culture.info/
CEU (Central European University – Budapest) — www.ceu.hu and CEU
    Center for Arts and Culture — www.ceu.hu/center_arts_culture.html
CIPAC (Congrès Interprofessionnel de l'Art Contemporain)
    — www.cipac.net
CIRCLE (Cultural Information and Research Centres Liason in Europe)
    — www.circle-network.org
CNC (Centro Nacional de Cultura – Lisbon) — www.cnc.pt
Comedia — www.comedia.org.uk
Commedia Network — www.comedianetwork.org
Cooperating Netherlands Foundations for Central and Eastern Europe
    — www.cooperatingnetherlandsfoundations.nl/index.htm
Council of Europe – Education – Culture and Heritage – Youth and Sport
    — www.coe.int/t/e/Cultural%5FCo-operation/
Council of Europe — www.coe.int
CPI (Cultural Policy Institute) — www.cpolicy.ru
Creative Exchange — www.creativexchange.org
Culture Programme 2000 – DG for Education and Culture of the European
    Commission — www.europa.eu.int/comm/culture/eac/index_en.html
Culturebase — www.culturebase.net
Culturelink Network — www.culturelink.org
Cultures France — www.culturesfrance.com

Ecumest — www.ecumest.ro

ENCATC (European Network of Cultural Administration Training Centres)
— www.encatc.org

ENICPA (European Network of Information Centres for the Performing Arts)
— www.enicpa.org

Euclid — www.euclid.info/

European Culture Portal — http://europa.eu.int/comm/culture

European Council of Artists — www.eca.dk

European Film Promotion — www.efp-online.com

European Forum for the Arts and Heritage — www.efah.org

European Institute for Progressive Cultural Policy — www.eipcp.net

European Opera Center — www.operaeuropa.com

European Parliament – Committee on Culture and Education
— www.europarl.eu.int/committees/cult_home.htm

European Parliament — www.europarl.eu.int

European Textile Network — www.etn-net.org

European Union National Institutes of Culture — www.eunic-europe.eu

European Writers' Congress — www.european-writers-congress.org

Europist — www.europist.net/

EUYO (European Union Youth Orchestra) — www.euyo.org.uk

Festival d'Avignon — www.festival-avignon.com

Festival dei due Mondi — www.spoletofestival.it

Festival Santarcangelo dei Teatri — www.santarcangelofestival.com

Finnish Cultural Institutes Abroad
— www.minedu.fi/minedu/inter_cooperation/fin_inst_abroad.html

Finnish Dance Information Center — www.danceinfo.fi

FIT (Festivals in Transition) — www.theatre-fit.org

Fondation de France — www.fdf.org

Fondation Roi Baudouin — www.kbs-frb.be

Fondazione Fitzcarraldo — www.fitzcarraldo.it

Fundação Calouste Gulbenkian — www.gulbenkian.pt

Giovanni Agnelli Foundation — www.fondazione-agnelli.it

Goethe-Institut — www.goethe.de

Golden Mask Performing Arts Festival
— www.theatre.ru/maska/eindex.html

Grand Theatre Groningen — www.grand-theatre.nl

Haus der Kulturen der Welt — www.hkw.de
Het Concertgebouw — www.concertgebouw.nl

ICOM (International Council of Museums) — www.icom.museum
ICOMOS (International Council on Monuments and Sites)
  — www.icomos.org
IETM (Informal European Theater Meetings) — www.ietm.org
IFACCA (International Federation of Arts Councils and Culture Agencies)
  — www.ifacca.org/ifacca2/en/default.asp
  and ACORNS (Arts and Culture Online Readers News Service)
  — www.ifacca.org/ifacca2/en/new/ page08_ACORNS.asp
IFEX (International Freedom of Expression Exchange) — www.ifex.org
IFLA (International Federation of Library Association) — www.ifla.org
IG Kultur Österreich — www.igkultur.at
IIE (Institut d'Etudes Européennes)
  — www.iee2.batb1.univ-paris8.fr/ iee/frame/cadres1.htm
  and Culture Europe — www.culture-europe.fr.fm/
IKSV (Istanbul Foundation for Culture and Arts) — www.iksv.org
In Place of War — www.inplaceofwar.net
INC (Institute of Network Culture) — www.networkcultures.org
INCD (International Network for Cultural Diversity) — www.incd.net
Info Relais — www.inforelais.org and — www.eu-inforelais.org
Institut für Auslandsbeziehungen — www.cms.ifa.de
  and Zeitschrift für Kultur Austausch
  — www.cms.ifa.de/zeitschrift_fuer_kulturaustausch. html?L=
Instituto Cervantes — www.cervantes.es
Inteatro Festival — www.inteatro.it
Intelligence on Culture — www.intelculture.org
Interarts Foundation — www.interarts.net
  and Cyberkaris — www.interarts. net/ cat/cyberkaris.html
Intercult — www.intercult.se
International Contemporary Art Network — http://ican.artnet.org/ican
International Dance Council
  — www.unesco.org/ngo/cid/html/directory.html
International İstanbul Theatre Festival — www.iksv.org/tiyatro
International Pen — www.internationalpen.org.uk
International Visegrad Fund — www.visegradfund.org
Istituti italiani di Cultura all'estero — www.esteri.it/ita/2_11_177.asp
ITI (International Theater Institute) — www.iti-worldwide.org

IVF (International Visegrad Fund) — www.visegradfund.org

Körber Stiftung — www.stiftung.koerber.de
Kulturkontakt — www.kulturkontakt.or.at
Kulturstiftung des Bundes — www.bundeskulturstiftung.de

La Caixa — www.lacaixa.es
La Compagnia di San Paolo — www.compagnia.torino.it
Laboratory for Culture — www.eurocult.org/lab or www.labforculture.org
LAF (Literature Across Frontiera) — www.lit-across-frontiers.org
    — www. mosaicpublishers.org and — www.transcript-review.org
Lambrakis Foundation — www.lrf.gr
Latvian Institute — www.li.lv
LEAD Network (Linked Euroregion Arts Development Network)
    — http://leadnetwork.nordpasdecalais.fr/
Les Pépinières européennes pour jeunes artistes — www.art4eu.net
Les Rencontres — www.lesrencontres.org
LIFT (London International Festival of Theatre) — www.liftfest.org.uk
Lithuanian Institute — www.lithuanianinstitute.lt

Manifesta International Foundation — www.manifesta.org
Maska — www.maska.si
Mediacult — www.mdw.ac.at/mediacult

NAI (Nederlands Architectuurinstituut) — www.nai.nl
Nederlandse Taalunie — www.taalunieversum.org
New Theater Institute of Latvia — www.theatre.lv
NewOp/NonOp — www.geocities.com/bdrogin/NewOp.html
NGO Global Network — www.ngo.org

OSCE (Organization for the Security and Cooperation in Europe)
    — www. osce.org
OISTAT (Organisation Internationale des Scènografes – Techniciens et Ar-
    chitectes de Théâtre) — www.oistat.org
ONDA — www.onda-international.com
On-the-Move — http://on-the-move.org
OPC (Observatoire des politiques culturelles – Grenoble)
    — www.observatoire-culture.net
Open Society Institute & Soros Foundation Network — www.soros.org

Platform Garanti Contemporary Art Center — www.platform.garanti.com.tr
Performing Arts Network Japan — www.performingarts.jp
Policies for Culture — www.policiesforculture.org/
Prince Claus Fund — www.princeclausfund.org
Prins Bernhard Cultuurfonds — www.prinsbernhardcultuurfonds.nl
ProCulture — www.proculture.cz
Pro Helvetia — www.pro-helvetia.ch

ResArtis — www.resartis.org
Robert Bosch Stiftung — www.bosch-stiftung.de
Romanian Cultural Institute — www.icr.ro

Salzburg Festival — www.salzburgfestival.at
Scottish Arts Council — www.scottisharts.org.uk
SIBMAS (Société Internationale des Bibliothèques et des Musées des Arts du
    Spectacle) — www.iti-sibmas.be
SIDA (Swedish Agency for International Development Cooperation)
    — www.sida.se
Siemens Arts Program
    — https://interhost.siemens.de/artsprogram/index.php
Sophiensæle — www.sophiensaele.de
Soros Foundation Network — www.soros.org
Spectre — http://post.openoffice.de/cgi-bin/mailman/listinfo/spectre
Spielart – Das Theaterfestival in München — www.spielart.org
Swedish Institute — www.si.se

Tanec Praha Festival — www.divadloponec.cz/tanec.php?lang=en
TEH (Trans Europe Halls) — www.teh.net
The A.G. Leventis Foundation — www.leventisfoundation.org
The Baltic Sea Culture Center — www.nck.org.pl
The Bank of Sweden Tercentenary Foundation — www.rj.se
The Danish Cultural Institute — www.dankultur.dk
The Felix Meritis Foundation — www.felix.meritis.nl
The Global Alliance for Cultural Diversity
    — www.unesco.org/culture/news-alliance/Anglais.htm
The Mondriaan Foundation — www.mondriaanfoundation.nl
The NGOs Network — www.ngos.net
The Power of Culture — www.powerofculture.nl/uk/index.html
The Red House — www.redhouse-sofia.org

The Swedish Institute — www.sweden.se
Theater a.d. Rühr — www.theater-an-der-ruhr.de
Théâtre Paris-Villette — www.theatre-paris-villette.com
THEOREM (Théâtres de l'Est et de l'Ouest – Rencontres Européennes du
    Millénaire — www.asso-theorem.com
TIN (Theater Instituut Nederland) — www.tin.nl
Trans Artist — www.transartists.nl

UN (United Nations) — http://www.un.org/
UNESCO (United Nations Educational – Scientific and Cultural Organiza-
    tion) — http://portal.unesco.org
Uniter (Theatre Union of Romania) — www.uniter.ro
Universes in Universe — http://universes-in-universe.de

Vaksa – The Sabanci Foundation — http://www.vaksa.org
Vebhi Koç Foundation — www.vkv.org.tr
VTI (Vlaams Theater Instituut) — www.vti.be
Victoria – a production house in Gent – Belgium — www.victoria.be
Villa Decius — www.villa.org.pl
Visegrad Fund — www.visegradfund.org

World Trade Organization — www.wto.org

Yapi Kredi Cultural Activities – Arts and Publishing
    — www.ykykultur. com.tr

ZfKF (Zentrum für Kulturforschung) — www.kulturforschung.de

KEY REFERENCES

Adorno, Theodor W. *Culture Industry. Selected Essays on Mass Culture.* London: Routledge, 2001.

Ahtisaari, Martti, et al. *Turkey in Europe? More than a Promise? Report of the Independent Commission on Turkey.* London and New York: British Council and Open Society Institute, 2004.

Alliès, Paul, Négrier, Emmanuel and Roche, François. *Pratiques des échanges culturels internationaux: les collectivités territoriales.* Paris: AFAA – Ministère des Affaires étrangères, 1994.

Anheier, Helmut and Isar, Yudhishthir Raj (eds). *Conflicts and Tensions.* The Culture and Globalization series, vol. 1. London: Sage, 2007.

Austen, Steve. *De Europese culturele ambitie. Amsterdam als metafoor.* Den Haag: SMO, 2004.

Autissier, Anne-Marie. *European Cultural Foundation 1954-2004.* Amsterdam: ECF, 2004.

Autissier, Anne-Marie. *L'Europe de la culture. Histoire(s) et enjeux.* Paris: Maison des cultures du monde, 2005.

Bakker, Han, et al. *Thinking forward.* Den Haag: FAPK & Mondriaan Foundation, 2004.

Bassler, Terrice and Wisse Smit, Mabel. *Building Donor Partnerships.* New York: Open Society Institute, 1997.

Bennett, Tony, et al. *Differing Diversities. Cultural Policy and Cultural Diversity.* Strasbourg: Council of Europe, 2001.

Bigger... Better... Beautiful? The Impact of the EU Enlargement on Cultural Opportunities Across Europe. Final Report of the conference organized in Budapest by Budapest Observatory, CCP Hungary and Euclide UK, 14-17 February 2002 (www.budobs.org/eu-conference.htm).

Birmant, Julie and Vimeux, Nathalie. (eds.). *Theatre East West.* Paris: Theorem, 2002.

Bloomfield, Jude and Bianchini, Franco. *Intercultural City. Planning for the Intercultural City*. Stroud: Comedia, 2004.

Bond, Kirsten, et al. *Cultural Diplomacy*. London: Demos, 2007.

Boorsma, Peter B., Hemel, A. van and Wielen, N. van der (eds.). *Privatization and Culture. Experiences in the Arts, Heritage and Cultural Industries in Europe*. Boston/Dordrecht/London: Kluwer Academic Publishers, 1998.

Caute, David. *The Dancer Defects. The Struggle for Cultural Supremacy During the Cold War*. Oxford: Oxford University Press, 2003.

Cliche, Danielle, et al. *Creative Europe. On the Governance and Management of Artistic Creativity in Europe*. Bonn: ERICarts, 2002.

Colloque d'experts. Dialogue au service de la communication interculturelle et inter-religieuse. Conclusions et synthèse analytique des débats. 7–9 octobre 2002. Strasbourg: Conseil de l'Europe, 2002.

Cools, Guy. "International co-production & touring." An IETM paper (www.ietm.org), 2004.

Cornu, Marie. *Compétences culturelles en Europe et principe de subsidiarité*. Bruxelles: Bruylant, 1993.

Council of Europe, *European Cultural Convention*, European Treaty Series 018, 1954 (http://conventions.coe.int/Treaty/EN/Treaties/Html/018.htm).

Consolidated Version of the Treaty Establishing The European Community, Official Journal C 325, 24 December 2002 (http://europa.eu.int/pol/reg/index_en.htm).

Delgado, Maria and Svich, Caridad (eds.). *Theatre in Crisis? Performance Manifestos for a New Century*. Manchester: Manchester University Press, 2002.

Demotte, Rudy. *Culture(s)*. Bruxelles: Editions Luc Pire, 2001.

European Cultural Foundation. *On the Road to a Cultural Policy for Europe*. Amsterdam: ECF, 2004.

The European Parliament's Ruffolo Report on cultural cooperation in the EU (200/2323(INI)). Drafted and adopted by the Committee on Culture, Youth, Education, the Media and Sport of the European Parliament, Rapporteur Giorgio Ruffolo, 16 July 2001 (http://www.europarl.eu.int/activities/archive/reports.do?language=EN).

Castells, Manuel. *The Rise of the Network Society*, vols. I–III. Oxford: Blackwell Publishers, 2000.

Convention on the Protection and Promotion of the Diversity of Cultural Expressions. Approved by the 33rd Session of the General Conference of UNESCO in Paris, 20 October 2005. (http://portal.unesco.org/culture/en/ev.php-url_id=29123&url_do=do_topic&url_section=201.html)

D'Angelo, Mario and Vespérini, Paul. *Cultural Policies in Europe: A Comparative Approach*. Strasbourg: Council of Europe, 1998.

Djian, Jean-Michel. *Politique culturelle: la fin d'un mythe*. Paris: Gallimard, 2005.

Dodd, Diane, Lyklema, Melle and Dittrich-Van Weringh, Kathinka. *A Cultural Component as an integral part of the EU's Foreign Policy?* Amsterdam: Boekman, 2006.

Dragičević-Šešić, Milena and Dragojević, Sanjin. *Arts management in turbulent times. Adaptable Quality Management*. Amsterdam: European Cultural Foundation and Boekmanstudies, 2005.

Engelander, Rudy and Klaic, Dragan (eds.). *Shifting Gears. Reflections and Reports on the Contemporary Performing Arts*. Amsterdam: Theater Instituut Nederland, 1998.

Europe Horizon Culture. Cinq ans après la chute du Mur. Rencontres internationales 5-6 novembre 1994. Synthèse des travaux. Paris: Ministère de la culture et de la francophonie, Département des affaires internationales, 1998.

Fisher, Rod. *A Cultural Dimension to the EU's External Policies. From Policy Statements to Practice and Potential*. Amsterdam: Boekmanstudies, 2007.

Grosjean, Etienne. *Quarante ans de coopération culturelle au Conseil de l'Europe, 1954-1994*. Strasbourg: Conseil de l'Europe, 1997.

Isar, Yudhishthir Raj (ed.). *Inclusive Europe: Horizon 2020*. Conference Reader. Budapest: Kulturpont iroda, 2005.

Fondazione Fitzcarraldo. *How Networking Works*. IETM Study on the Effects of Networking. Helsinki: Arts Council of Finland, 2001. (www.ietm.org/docs/ietmeng.pdf)

Fondazione Fitzcarraldo. *Cultural Cooperation in Europe: What Role for the Foundations?* Brussels: NEF, 2004. (www.fitzcarraldo.it)

Gordon, Christopher and Mundy, Simon. *European Perspectives on Cultural Policy*. Paris: UNESCO, 2001.

Hlavajova, Maria and Winder, Jill (eds.). *Who if Not We Should at Least Try to Imagine the Future of All This?* Amsterdam: Artimo, 2004.

Hurkmans, Ben, et al. (eds.). *All that Dutch. International Cultural Politics*. Rotterdam: NAi Publishers, 2005.

In from the margins. A Contribution to the Debate on Culture and Development in Europe. Strasbourg: Council of Europe, 1997.

Janssen, Ingrid, et al. (eds.). *A Portrait of the Artist 2015. Artistic Careers and Higher Education in Europe*. Amsterdam: Boekmanstudies, 2004.

Kaufmann, Therese and Raunig, Gerald. *Anticipating European Cultural Policies*. Wien: EIPCP, 2003.

Klaic, Dragan. *Reform or Transition. The Future of the Repertory Theatre in Central and Eastern Europe*. New York: Open Society Institute, 1997.

Klaic, Dragan. *Europe as a Cultural Project*. Amsterdam: European Cultural Foundation, 2005. (also on www.eurocult.org/publications).

Langeveld, H. M. *Kunst op termijn. Toekomst-scenario's voor cultuurbeleid*. 2000. Amsterdam/Den Haag: Boekmanstudies/ Sociaal en Cultureel Planbureau.

Lavrijsen, Ria (ed.). *Cultural Diversity in the Arts*. Amsterdam: Royal Tropical Institute, 1993.

Lind, Maria and Minichbauer, Raimund (eds.). *European Cultural Policies 2015. A Report with Scenarios on the Future of Public Funding for Contemporary Art in Europe*. Stockholm: Laspis, 2005.

Lombard, Alain. *Politique culturelle internationale. Le modèle française face à la mondialisation*. Paris: Maison des cultures du monde, 2003.

Maass, Kurt-Juergen (ed.). *Kultur und Aussenpolitik. Handbuch für Studium und Praxis*. Baden-Baden: Nomos Verlag, 2005.

Mattelart, Armand. *Diversité cuturelle et mondialisation*. Paris: La Decouverte, 2005.

Miller, Toby and Yudice, George. *Cultural Policy*. London: Sage, 2002.

Mundy, Simon. *Making it Home. Europe and the Politics of Culture*. Amsterdam: European Cultural Foundation, 1997.

Obuljen, Nina. *Why we need European cultural policies. The Impact of the EU enlargement on cultural policies in transition countries*. Amsterdam: European Cultural Foundation, 2006.

Obuljen, Nina and Smiers, Joost (eds.). *UNESCO Convention on the Protection and Promotion of the Diversity of Cultural Expressions: Making It Work*. Zagreb: Institute for International Relations, 2006. Culturlink 9.

Palmer, Robert. *European Cities and Capitals of Culture. Study Prepared for the European Commission*. Brussels, 2004. (www.eu.int/comm/culture/eac/ sources_info/ studies/pdf_word/cap_part1.pdf).

Palmer, Robert and Gordon, Christopher (eds.). *Culture and European Regions. Preliminary research into regional cultural policy*. An EFAH study. Lille: Conseil regional Nord-Pas de Calais, 2004.

Pérez de Cuéllar, Javier, et al. *Our Creative Diversity. Report of the World Commission on Culture and Development*. Paris: UNESCO, 1996.

"The Politics of Intercultural. Myths, Realities and Dreams. Sweden 1991–2001". *Korsdrag*, 4–5. 2001.

Regourd, Serge. *L'Exception culturelle*. Paris: PUF, 2002.

Saunders, Francis Stonor. *Who Paid the Piper*. London: Granta, 2000.

Smiers, Joost. *The Role of the European Community Concerning the Cultural Article 151 in the Treaty of Amsterdam*. Utrecht: Utrecht School of the Arts, 2002.

Smiers, Joost. *Arts Under Pressure. Promoting Cultural Diversity in the Age of Globalization*. London: Zed Books, 2003.

Steinert, Heinz. *Culture Industry*. Cambridge: Polity, 2003. (Orig. *Kulturindustrie*, Muenster: Westfaelisches Dampfboot, 1998).

Study on Cultural Cooperation in Europe. Report for the European Commission. Brussels: Europan Forum for the Arts and Heritage and Interarts, 2003. (www.eu.int/comm/culture/eac/sources_info/pdf-word/summary_report_coop_cult.pdf)

Švob-Djokić, Nada. *Cultural Transitions in South-East Europe*. Zagreb: Institute for International Relations, 2004.

Ten Cate, Ritsaert. *Man Looking for Words*. Amsterdam: Theater Instituut Nederland, 1996.

Universal Declaration on Cultural Diversity, Adopted by the 31st Session of the General Conference of UNESCO in Paris, 2 November 2001 (http://unesdoc.unesco.org/images/0012/001271/127160m.pdf).

Weeda, Hanneloes, Suteu, Corina and Smithuijsen, Cas (eds.). *The Arts, Politics and Change. Participative Cultural Policy-Making in South East Europe*. Amsterdam: ECF, Ecumest Association & Boekmanstudies, 2005.

Wend Fenton, Rose de and Neal, Lucy. *The Turning World. Stories from the London International Festival of Theatre*. London: Calouste Gulbenkian Foundation UK, 2005.

Williams, Raymond. *Key Words*. London: Fontana, 1976.

ACKNOWLEDGMENT

This book was written and published thanks to the generous support of Stichting Internationale Culturele Activiteiten (www.sica.nl), a Dutch platform for international cultural cooperation. The material in this book has been developed in many courses, seminars and workshops that I have been giving for years and especially at the Amsterdam-Maastricht Summer University, Marcel Hicter Foundation European Diploma in Cultural Management, Leiden University Faculty of Creative and Performing Arts, Central European University, University of Bologna GIOCA master program and others. Some ideas and stances have been previously tested in conference speeches and articles.

The practice, reflection and concrete examples of numerous colleagues, participants and students have enriched me greatly in my insights and stances. Several international cultural networks provided a steady flow of news, developments, ingenious projects and often fascinating discussions. I have been especially stimulated by my long lasting involvement with the IETM, by serving as a board member and President of EFAH, by close and various collaborations with the European Cultural Foundation and the Open Society Institute.

Numerous friends and colleagues offered valuable criticism and suggestions on how to improve this manuscript. Among them, Milena Dragičević Šešić, Christopher Gordon, Ruud Engelander, Ugo Bacchella, Anne Marie Autissier, Lidia Varbanova and Raj Isar offered their expertise and time with exceptional generosity. The greater part of the book I wrote in Istanbul, while on a research stay, supported by the Dutch Fonds voor amateur- en podiumkunsten (www.fapk.nl) and enjoying the kind hospitality of Prof. Dr. Selcuk Erez.

My research assistant Lucia Babina gathered much data and checked and rechecked names, titles and facts. Dessi Gavrilova of the Center for Arts and Culture of the Central European University and Péter Inkei and János

Zoltán Szabó of the Budapest Observatory found practical ways to turn the manuscript into a book. Finally, my family put up valiantly with my frequent absences from home, on many weekends when I was away on the international cultural pursuits that provided the experiential foundation of this book.

D. K.

ABOUT THE AUTHOR

Dragan Klaic is a theater scholar and cultural analyst. He serves as a Permanent Fellow of Felix Meritis Foundation in Amsterdam and teaches Arts and Cultural Policy at the Leiden University. He lectures widely at various universities, speaks at conferences and symposia and serves as advisor, editor, columnist, researcher and trainer. His fields of engagement are contemporary performing arts, European cultural policies, strategies for cultural development and international cultural cooperation, interculturalism and cultural memory.

Educated in dramaturgy in Belgrade and with a doctorate in theater history and dramatic criticism from Yale University, Klaic worked as a theater critic and dramaturg, held professorships at the University of Arts Belgrade and University of Amsterdam and guest professorships in the USA, led the Theater Instituut Nederland, co-founded the European Theater Quarterly *Euromaske*, and served as the President of the European Network of Information Centers for the Performing Arts and of the European Forum for the Arts and Heritage. He was the Moderator of the Reflection Group of the European Cultural Foundation (2002–2004) and authored its final report, *Europe as a Cultural Project* (Amsterdam: ECF, 2005). He is the initiator and Chair of the European Festival Research Project, an interdisciplinary consortium for the study of the current festivalization of daily life. In the fall of 2005 he studied the emerging alternative cultural infrastructure in Istanbul and its connectivity with EU cultural systems, resulting in an analytical report, *Istanbul's Cultural Constellation and Its European Prospects* (2006). In 2007 he was a Visiting Professor at the Central European University in Budapest and at the University of Bologna, and a Research Fellow at the Collegium Budapest.

Among his books are several works published in the former Yugoslavia before 1991, as well as *Terrorism and Modern Drama* (co-edited with J. Orr, Edinburgh Univ. Press, 1990, paperback 1992), *The Plot of The Future: Utopia and Dystopia in Modern Drama* (Michigan Univ. Press, 1991), *Shifting Gears/*

169

Changer de vitesse (co-edited with R. Englander, TIN Amsterdam, 1998) and most recently an exile memoir *Exercises in Exile,* published in Dutch (*Thuis is waar je vrienden zijn. Ballingschap tussen Internet en Ikeatafel,* Amsterdam: Cossee, 2004) and in Croatian. Klaic's articles and columns appeared in many periodicals and in over 50 edited books in several languages. He is a Contributing Editor of the *Theater* magazine (USA) and member of several advisory boards in Budapest, Brussels and The Hague.

PUBLICATION PARTNERS

Center for Arts and Culture (CAC)

The Center for Arts and Culture (CAC) at the Central European University (CEU) was established in 2003 with the aim to stimulate research and curricula development in the field of arts & culture and cultural policy, to stir culture-related debate within the university, and to provide the CEU community with an inspiring artistic program that would bring together students from all disciplines, academic staff and Budapest citizens. CAC activity covers two main projects:

Artistic Projects • CAC organizes in-house artistic events at CEU that are aimed at bringing an additional dimension to the experience of studying at the University—an artistic dimension that is there to remind us about what makes the world spin.

Academic Projects • CAC invites outstanding cultural scholars to hold culture-related public lectures, seminars, or roundtable discussions with representatives of the academic community. The center aims at introducing culture-related curricula and research at CEU. Through these activities CAC makes sure that culture stays high on the University agenda. For more information go to: www.cac.ceu.hu

SICA (Service Centre for International Cultural Activities)

The SICA is the Netherlands' supporting organization for international cultural exchange. SICA provides information and advice pertinent to all cultural sectors and disciplines, regarding specific countries, activities, sources for financial support, available networks and a range of practical concerns. Working together with foundations, cultural institutes and the government, SICA helps promote international dissemination of Dutch art and culture by developing and coordinating a wide range of programs in both the Netherlands and abroad.

The Netherlands European Cultural Contact Point (CCP) is part of the SICA helpdesk, providing information about European cultural grants, notably those stipulated in the Culture program. www.sica.nl

Regional Observatory on Financing Culture in East-Central Europe
(The Budapest Observatory, BO)

The Budapest Observatory was created in 1999 with the support of the Hungarian National Commission for Unesco, in response to the call of the Unesco world conference in 1998 in Stockholm for systematic monitoring of processes of cultural policy all over the world. The mission of the Observatory is to be of help to those, who want to know more about the ways culture is being administered and financed in East-Central European countries. The Observatory has been conducting analyses, surveys and research in its remit, in most cases of a comparative character. Some of these have been commissioned by international, others by national agencies, again others done on our own initiative. One of the most successful projects of the Observatory hitherto has been our decisive role in organizing Inclusive Europe? - Horizon 2020, in November 2006 in Budapest: a ministerial conference combined with the annual meeting of the European Forum for the Arts and Heritage. Our monthly newsletter reaches nearly 2000 addresses all over Europe. For more information go to: www.budobs.org

EUCLID (www.euclid.info)

EUCLID is an independent agency providing European & international information, research and consultancy services to the arts and cultural sector.

It provides an extensive range of online information resources through Culture. Info (see www.culture.info). There are a number of individual web pages, including:

- funding (including detailed information on opportunities from the EU),
- partner search,
- directories of cultural contacts in around 100 countries in Europe and internationally,
- a video clips service (a "cultural YouTube") for the cultural sector (via http:// preview.culture.info).

Other EUCLID services include its free Alert e-newsletter on EU funding and other opportunities, an extensive program of seminars and conferences, and research and consultancy projects—past clients include the European Commission, the European Parliament, government departments in several European countries including Hungary and Malta, and many agencies and organizations in the UK, including the British Council and Arts Council England.

Lightning Source UK Ltd.
Milton Keynes UK
UKOW06n2150160415

249771UK00004B/52/P